Women's Sovereignty and Body Autonomy Beyond Roe v. Wade

Girl God Books

Edited by Arlene Bailey,
Pat Daly, Sharon Smith,
and Trista Hendren

Cover Art by Ravynne M. Phelan

www.thegirlgod.com

Girl God Books

Re-visioning Medusa: from Monster to Divine Wisdom

A remarkable collection of essays, poems, and art by scholars who have researched Her, artists who have envisioned Her, and women who have known Her in their personal story. All have spoken with Her and share something of their communion in this anthology.

In Defiance of Oppression – The Legacy of Boudicca

An anthology that encapsulates the Spirit of the defiant warrior in a modern apathetic age. No longer will the voices of our sisters go unheard, as the ancient Goddesses return to the battlements, calling to ignite the spark within each and every one of us—to defy oppression wherever we find it, and stand together in solidarity.

Warrior Queen: Answering the Call of The Morrigan

A powerful anthology about the Irish Celtic Goddess. Each contributor brings The Morrigan to life with unique stories that invite readers to partake and inspire them to pen their own. Included are essays, poems, stories, chants, rituals, and art from dozens of story-tellers and artists from around the world, illustrating and recounting the many ways this powerful Goddess of war, death, and prophecy has changed their lives.

Inanna's Ascent: Reclaiming Female Power

Inanna's Ascent examines how females can rise from the underworld and reclaim their power, sovereignly expressed through poetry, prose and visual art. All contributors are extraordinary women in their own right, who have been through some difficult life lessons—and are brave enough to share their stories.

Original Resistance: Reclaiming Lilith, Reclaiming Ourselves

There is, perhaps, no more powerful archetype of female resistance than Lilith. As women across the globe rise up against the patriarchy, Lilith stands beside them, misogyny's original challenger. This anthology—a chorus of voices hitting chords of defiance, liberation, anger and joy—reclaims the goodness of women bold enough to hold tight to their essence.

The Crone Initiation: Women Speak on the Menopause Journey

The Crone Initiation is an anthology of women's experiences of perimenopause and menopause, and the part Goddess plays in this journey. Crone's presence in the breakdowns and breakthroughs, the disintegration and rebuilding, is expressed through words and art. Meaning is reclaimed and the power of the Elder restored.

Re-Membering with Goddess: Healing the Patriarchal Perpetuation of Trauma

Re-Membering with Goddess is an anthology of women's experiences of trauma—trauma as a result of patriarchy; trauma perpetuated by patriarchy; and how through personal healing of trauma the Goddess is re-membered, re-embodied and resurrected. As repeating loops of trauma restriction release—in the mind, body and nervous system—Goddess is re-embodied and rises... and the patriarchy falls.

Just as I Am: Hymns Affirming the Divine Female

What is a Hermnal? It's the collective sigh of our ancestral Grandmothers. It's a means of drawing us closer together as Sisters. It is a compilation of songs that affirm our Sacredness, apart from Man, and assures us that we are Sovereign Beings and Creatrixes, too. And it is our Love Gift of Gratitude to Mama.

Willendorf's Legacy: The Sacred Body

Travel through time and discover a world where the fullness of women was both admired and deified. Reclaim your beautiful Goddess body through the rich pages of this powerful collection of art, poetry and essays celebrating our divine inheritance as daughters of Willendorf.

The Girl God

A book for children young and old, celebrating the Divine Female by Trista Hendren. Magically illustrated by Elisabeth Slettnes with quotes from various faith traditions and feminist thinkers.

Complete list of Girl God publications at www.thegirlgod.com

"To rid ourselves of this system is the only way to become free. Freedom for women will never be achieved unless they unite into an organized political force powerful enough and conscious enough and dynamic enough to truly represent half of society."

-Nawal El Saadawi, *The Hidden Face of Eve*

Dedication:

We dedicate this anthology to all the girls and women in the past – and those today – who have suffered due to misogynistic laws that deny women both their bodily autonomy and their sovereignty.

We mourn all the women who've lost their lives due to backstreet abortions.

We mourn for all the girls around the world that are forced into Clitoridectomies, losing their body sovereignty and personal choice.

We honor the doctors and workers who risk their lives on the front lines in abortion clinics, all the women who fight via marches, writing, painting, and teaching.

We devote this book to all the girls yet to have their first menses who will come of age in this massively dystopian environment.

This work is at its core a clarion call for women's body autonomy and sovereignty with abortion rights as only one part of a larger global problem.

Table of Contents

Why is Roe v. Wade So Important for Women Everywhere?

Sharon Smith

As the USA and the world struggle with the ramifications of the Supreme Court decision to overturn Roe v. Wade, many questions need to be asked—and answered—about the implications of this ruling. But first, we must be clear on just what has transpired. Many people think that Roe v. Wade was exclusively about a woman's right to an abortion, but this ruling affects much more than terminating a pregnancy.

It also has to do with one's right to privacy:

> *The case was brought by Norma McCorvey—known by the legal pseudonym "Jane Roe"—who in 1969 became pregnant with her third child. McCorvey wanted an abortion, but she lived in Texas where abortion was illegal, except when necessary to save the mother's life. Her attorneys, Sarah Weddington and Linda Coffee, filed a lawsuit on her behalf in U.S. Federal Court against her local district attorney, Henry Wade, alleging that Texas' abortion laws were unconstitutional. A special three-judge court of the U.S. District Court for the Northern District of Texas heard the case and ruled in her favor. The parties appealed this ruling to the Supreme Court.* [Wikipedia]

> On January 22, 1973, the Supreme Court ruled that *"the Due Process Clause of the Fourteenth Amendment to the U.S. Constitution provides a fundamental 'right to privacy' that protects a pregnant woman's liberty to abort her fetus. The right is not absolute, and has to be balanced against the government's interest in protecting women's health and protecting prenatal life. Texas' statutes making it a crime to procure an abortion violated this right."*

On June 24, 2022, the Supreme Court overruled Roe in Dobbs v. Jackson Women's Health Organization on the grounds that the substantive right to abortion was not "deeply rooted in this Nation's history or tradition", nor considered a right when the Due Process Clause was ratified in 1868, and was unknown in U.S. law until Roe. This view was disputed by some legal historians and criticized by the dissenting opinion, which argued that many other rights—contraception, interracial marriage, and same-sex marriage—did not exist when the Due Process Clause was ratified in 1868, and thus were unconstitutional by the Dobbs majority's logic. The decision was supported and opposed by the anti-abortion and abortion-rights movements in the United States, respectively, and was generally condemned by international observers and foreign leaders. [Wikipedia]

Why is this important?

Because when a person's right to privacy—in this case, a woman's right to bodily autonomy and the freedom to choose whether or not to carry a pregnancy full term, is challenged and rejected by the courts—especially the highest court in the land—then what is next? What other rights will we forfeit?

Since the overturn of Roe v. Wade, many women and girls have suffered the physical, mental and emotional ramifications of such oppressive laws: Some have already died from lack of proper treatment, because doctors are now afraid to perform abortions, even when they are necessary, due to the threat of lawsuits by their states and, perhaps, the loss of their medical licenses or the possibility of going to jail. Many other women have almost died because of current concern among physicians and their hesitation to get involved in anything abortion-related. In mid-July, the case of a 10-year-old Ohio girl, raped and impregnated by a 26-year-old man, came to national and world attention when she was denied the right to an abortion in her home state of Ohio, which has made abortions, even in the case of rape or incest, illegal. Her parents were forced to take her out of state to Indiana to have the procedure done safely.

President Joe Biden had this to say during remarks on reproductive care and abortion access:

> *"Ten years old. Raped, six weeks pregnant. Already traumatized. Was forced to travel to another state. Imagine being that little girl, forced to give birth to a rapist's child. I can't think of anything as much more extreme."*

Add to that the GOP's attempts to deny women (especially poor women of color) the right to birth control. One-hundred-ninety-five Republicans voted against the Right to Contraception Act in July of 2022. The bill passed in the House by a final vote of 195 to 228. Only 8 Republicans voted for it. In 2024, the bill was blocked by Republicans in the Senate. The bill has been tabled under the current administration. And then, we have a Supreme Court that, according to *The Guardian:*

> *"is a court that has been constructed to thwart the will of the people with the help of hundreds of millions in rightwing dark money, by playing brutalist constitutional hardball ripped from the autocrat's handbook, and by exploiting the same structural inequities in redistricting, the US Senate and the electoral college that helped protect slavery and then Jim Crow. This supreme court has now placed itself above the people and above the law. Simply because they have the power. Simply because they can."*[1]

With Far Right Conservative Republicans currently in control of the Supreme Court, and pandering to Far Right Conservative Christians who want this government to establish Christianity as the national religion, and biblical morals as the Law of the Land, will they use their power to "re-interpret the law"? Nancy Pelosi (D-CA), Speaker of the House, said this at a news conference before the vote took place:

> *"It is clear that their attempts to roll back the clock on contraception is again another plank on their extreme agenda*

---

[1] Daley, David. "Republicans have hijacked the US supreme court. It's time to expand it," The Guardian; Jun 27, 2022.

for American women. Let us be clear: We are not going back —
for our daughters, for our granddaughters."

We are living in difficult times here in America. But we're not alone. Women all around the world are suffering under repressive patriarchal regimes. We must, all of us, stay on guard. Any nation that blatantly oppresses its women is a nation that has become dangerously imbalanced. If ever there was a time for women to come together, stand together, *rebel* together, it is now. We must put aside our differences and embrace our common experiences as women and, more than that, as *sisters*.

Roe v. Wade is a wake-up call, here in America, a clarion bell sounding yet another assault by Patriarchy upon girls and women. We can either sit silently, do nothing, and watch as we're ushered into a Handmaid's Tale Dystopia... Or we can rise up in our Divine Feminine fury and work tirelessly to bring the Beast of Patriarchy down.

It's up to us. It seems a great burden, I know. But let's take heart in the fact that we are not alone. We are surrounded by countless ancestral grandmothers, aunts and cousins; women who came before us and stood their ground, fighting for the rights we still DO have today. Let us draw strength from the knowledge that they did not give up; they did not give in. And let us, in their spirit, go forth and do likewise.

"When sleeping women waken, mountains move," declares a Chinese proverb.

It's time, Sisters, to raise Boudicca's sword and let her guttural battle cry propel us forward as the tidal wave of Woman Rage rises!

Boudicca

Andrea Redmond

About this Anthology

Trista Hendren

Women's Sovereignty and Body Autonomy Beyond Roe v. Wade contains a variety of writing styles from women around the world. Various forms of English are included in this anthology and we chose to keep spellings of the writers' place of origin to honor/ honour each individual's unique voice.

It was the express intent of the editors to not police standards of citation, transliteration, and formatting. Contributors have determined which citation style, italicization policy and transliteration system to adopt in their pieces. The resulting diversity is a reflection of the diverse academic fields, genres and personal expressions represented by the authors.[2]

If you find that a particular writing doesn't sit well with you, please feel free to use the Al-Anon suggestion: "Take what you like, leave the rest!" That said, if there aren't at least several pieces that challenge you, we have not done our job here.

Please note that none of the information presented in this book is meant to replace the advice of a medical, health, legal and/or any other professional or service. How you choose to act on the words and content is of your own determination and free will.

Each contributor is on a different part of her journey. The beauty of anthologies is the variety of perspectives they are able to hold within one book. I often find that the pieces and language that are most uncomfortable for me hold the keys to parts of myself I have yet to look at.

---

[2] This paragraph is borrowed and adapted with love from *A Jihad for Justice: Honoring the Work and Life of Amina Wadud.* Edited by Kecia Ali, Juliane Hammer and Laury Silvers.

We are in a transition these last decades with language, and I have seen a lot of arguments around this—even with people who mostly agree with each other. Personally, I try to just listen to what the writer is trying to say. The fact remains that few of us were privileged with a woman-affirming education—and we all have a lot of time to make up for. Let's all be gentle with each other through this process.

I have a tradition of sitting down to read the entire anthology in one sitting when I receive the first proof copy. This is not a book to do that with. It is heavy – and a **trigger warning** is advisable for much of the writing. Take good care of yourself as you read these pages.

We welcome you to join us in the circle of 44 women who have contributed to this book—as we reclaim our sovereignty.

Magic and Mystery: Answering Her Call
Arlene Bailey

We are a Nation at War with its Women

Arlene Bailey

Some would say we are a nation at war with itself. That's not true. We are a nation under patriarchy that is at war with its women.

All bodily rights of a woman born woman are now under a legislated legal system. There is no body autonomy for a woman born woman. She may not decide if she gets pregnant to birth or not birth for that is now a decision the court has already made for her. No matter "how" the insemination occurred, according to the law she will birth that child. She has NO rights to her own body. She has NO rights to any decision or wish with regard to her body. She has no recourse for an unwanted pregnancy, at least no legal way out.

Patriarchy has declared war on the American woman, but what they don't realize is we will go to battle for the rights of sovereignty and body autonomy. We will go to war screeching, "the patriarchy does not control our bodies". We will go to war with the resolve of Lilith not to bow to patriarchal demands and the battle cry of Boudicca as she lays waste to those that would dare to control her body as they raped her, raped her daughters. We will fly with the wings of Raven as the Morrigan picks the flesh of the dead. We will NOT be controlled or dismissed!

It's not about whether the decision to terminate a pregnancy is right or wrong, not about abortion. It IS about a woman's right – an inalienable right – to decide for herself... to choose for herself... what is right and good and holy for her and HER body. It's about this decision belonging ONLY to Her!

We are a nation at war with its women. We are a nation where the bulk of the male population does not see a woman's body as holy and sacred and sovereign. Rather, they say a woman's body is something to be owned, something to be regulated, something to be controlled. Something that is meant only for man's pleasure or to birth a child.

Women have NO CHOICE in this and we are nothing if not akin to prisoners.

Already there are cults in this nation who dictate how a woman dresses. Cults who dictate when a woman may or may not have sexual relations and with whom. Cults who dictate when a woman may do anything and how she may do it.

Roe v. Wade – or rather the eradication of Roe v. Wade, while seemingly only about once again making abortions illegal – is really about body sovereignty. It is about who controls that sovereignty and right now that control belongs NOT to a woman but to the patriarchy.

But what the patriarchy – mostly men but also many women – does not realize is *we will not surrender willingly.* We will not just give over the control of our bodies to a piece of paper written by men, legislated by men and put into law by men and one woman.

I am no longer a bleeding woman, no longer a woman with a uterus, no longer a woman who can birth a child and still I am outraged. If truth be known, I am fearful for those younger women who do still bleed and release eggs and can get pregnant and can birth a child. By law, they have now lost ALL autonomy over their own bodies! They have lost all control over what happens to their bodies should they get pregnant and, the truth of the matter is that the fictional work known as *The Handmaid's Tale* hovers on the horizon as the new life for ALL women, not only those who can still birth. Read this again! In a world akin to that of the fictional writing, *A Handmaid's Tale*, ALL women will lose body autonomy and sovereignty.

I wonder how many women in this country, in the United States of America, realize just how close reality is mimicking fiction? Do they realize – these younger women, the women who can still give birth – that the government now owns and controls their uteruses, controls even what happens to the children who are stirring within?

I am ANGRY for these women. I am FEARFUL for these women, and, in truth, I am fearful for all women not just in the United States but around the world. Many countries already have these types of laws and their women have little to no control over their own bodies. It's a disease that is crawling across our land, making its way around the globe, tying up and burning down women's rights.

How soon will the women of the world have no rights, no body autonomy, no right to make any decision with regard to the children they carry or even perhaps the children they want? How soon will they have no rights to ANY part of their bodies or ANY part of their lives?

How long before women's bodies are controlled to the point that we are told how to dress and act – for when Roe v. Wade was originally put into law, it was not just about pregnancy and abortion. It opened up a world to women with regard to how they clothed themselves, how they appeared in public, how they appeared in private. That level of sovereignty and body autonomy is now becoming just a memory.

Perhaps the worst of this shift in attitude and in law is that an unborn fetus – an entity that cannot exist on its own – now has MORE rights than any woman who is still able to get pregnant – and the virus that is patriarchy is reaching for more. Already I am seeing the shift in clothing and how a woman may appear in private or public. Take a walk through a clothing store or look online and see how many long skirts and prairie dresses are now offered. Clothing that was once called matronly. Look closer at shoes once called matronly that now sit next to the sexy sandal. Oh yes, the other is still there but it is becoming less the dominant message. Rather the new message is *cover up*. Sure, you'll have the short skirts and crop tops and bikinis for a while but this shift in appearance is happening.

Pay attention women, for the insidious fingers of patriarchy are encroaching on every aspect of our lives – and control is their goal. Religious history – and the sky god who kicked Lilith out of the garden, replacing her with a woman made from man – is their guide and teacher and leader of their army. The insidiousness of patriarchy just got bigger and it's aiming its arrows of control and death at women. In the US, there are states creating legislation that make women nothing more than chattel and they are coming for the rest of us.

I am an old woman and a woman who fought for women's rights – not just about abortion, but about the right for a woman to have a bank account in her own name, the right to own property in her own name, the right to NOT take her husband's name if married and so much more. I am a woman who fought for these rights and there were so many women who came before me who also fought. A perfect example is the women known as Suffragettes who fought and won the legal right for women to vote.

When I look now, I wonder where are the women who will stand and fight? Oh yes, there are those of us who are fighting this and there are those who are on the frontlines of this fight, but there are also those who sit at home or in offices asking, "Well, what can I do?" So, they do nothing.

So, I ask you this... How important is the control of your own body? How important is the ability to choose the clothing you like no matter what it looks like? How important is the freedom to come and go as you please? I ask this because patriarchy is coming for all of these and more – and the freedom for women to express themselves in whatever way they choose now hovers around the chopping block. With the Supreme Court we now have – a court controlled by the religious right and those men and women who would have ALL women return to nothing more than chattel – THAT Supreme Court is currently looking at all the laws around women (including reading laws as far back as the 1500's) and their goals are eradication of any and all freedom for a woman.

Don't believe me? Research Justice Alito and see how many laws he is looking at that are hundreds of years old... how many laws he is looking at as precedent for changing the current laws around women!

Some would say we are a nation at war with itself. That's not true. We are a nation under patriarchy that is at war with its women.

CRESCENDO
Cheryl Braganza

Those Witches they Burned

Maya Luna

Those Witches they Burned
Were Gynaecologists

Midwife
Doula
Abortionist
Miscarriage Tender
Pregnancy Preventer
Medicine Carrier
Potion Bottle Herb and
Womb

The Ones who Knew
That Secret Incantation
The mysteries
Of the blood
Of Incarnation

Body of Woman
Most Ancient Temple
Original Church
The First Place of
Worship and
Reverence

Body of Woman
Bridge between
Spirit and Matter
Pulling Souls Down to
Earth
Stitching Divine
Into Flesh

Body of Woman
That Swelling of tide that
Sheds and Dies
Grows and Births
Feeds Life and
Kills Life
Right between
Her Thighs

Body of Woman
Turning cycles with the
Moon
Endless Throb of Creation
Portal between
The Two Worlds

Is it any wonder?
That the witches they burned
For tending to this temple
Of relentless power
And aching divinity
Were also devotees of
The Goddess?

Goddess of Moon
Goddess of Snake
Goddess of Earth and
Dirt
Booming your orgasming
Birth
Screaming Love into
Being
Singing us all to our
Death

Radical Realm of
Impermanence
Incarnation and Immanence

Snake
Sheds Skin
Moon
Sheds Skin
Womb
Sheds Skin

All matter sheds skin
As it blossoms blooms and
Dies

Matter which means
Mother

Mother of Life
We have visioned you only
In the Light
Generous, self-sacrificing
Face of the Feminine
Sweet Gentle Mother
Of Yes
We have tried to banish your other
Face

Mother of Death
Dark Mother of Destruction
Miscarriage
Menstruation
And even
Abortion

We forgot
A good Mother knows when to say
No

We forgot how to bow our heads
Low
To the sacred act
Of letting go

Body of Woman
We fear what you know
About Existence

But the witches knew
The midwives knew
How to Anoint
That Round Bellied One
Who is both Light and Dark
Life and Death
Who Churns Time
Who both Gives and
Takes Away

They've tried to break our backs
To bow
For 5000 years

To worship the idols
Of Transcendence
To forsake the
Sacred Immanent
Repent our sins to the Fathers for
Forgiveness
Who say they are pro life
Yet know nothing of
The vital mysteries of
Creation

The Witches knew
God was no Man
That's why they had to
Burn

Body of Woman
You are the place they cannot wash out
Cannot erase
Cannot get clean
You are the terrifying reminder
Of everything we wish to
Forget

Body of Woman
Sanctuary of Beginnings
Fertile Ground of Sacred Endings

You are the Whole Truth
Of the Nature of Reality
You are Holy Darkness
Bleeding Into
Holy Light

Body of Woman
Whose power is beyond all power
Whose power has been
Envied
Scorned
Hated
Vilified
Demonized
Tortured
and Traumatized

Body of Woman
You are the Soft Pink
And Tender Place

Where Violence and War
Has been waged
Where the religion of
Unfathomable Love
Became the place of
Abominable Domination

Body of Woman
Your body has been made
Not your own

Body of woman
They tried to take the
Goddess out of You

Witch and Stitch and Potion
Herb and Blood and Baptism

Body of Woman
Bridge between
Spirit and Matter
Vessel of the
Two Worlds
Holy Portal of
Life and Death

Forgive us Mother
For we know not what we do

Lilith Rising

Arlene Bailey

Declaration of American Women's Independence

Pamela Genghini Munoz

When in the course of human events, six justices of the U.S. Supreme Court commit perjury and reverse a decision they swore under oath they would not touch;

When in doing so, the only laws they can cite for support date back to The Burning Times;

When the governments instilled upon the Earth no longer derive their powers justly or from the consent of the governed;

A decent respect to the women whose rights have been trampled requires that we give voice to the causes which impel them to burn the fucking house down.

We hold these truths whether they're evident to those in power or not:

That all humans are created equal, inside the bodies of women.

That the Goddess has endowed women with the sacred ability to bring souls from the spirit realm into this one.

That this sacred task likewise bestows on women certain inalienable rights, among these:

The right to decide if, and how many, souls she will usher into this world;

The right to decide who will be the earthly father to each of her human children;

The right to decide not to bring a human life into this world, for whatever reason speaks to her.

That men neither house the microcosm of the universe that is a womb in their bodies,

nor face the danger, labor, and pain it takes to bear a child,

and therefore have no authority on which to dictate to women what choice they should make when it comes to bearing children.

Therefore, we the women of the United States of America, hereby declare this betrayal to be an extension of unwarrantable jurisdiction over our bodies.

That this betrayal demands that we seek out redress and wage justice.

And for the support of this declaration, with a firm reliance on ourselves and our sisters, we pledge that those in power and their enablers shall know no peace until justice is obtained and our rights are vindicated.

And in the words of our sisters,

Be thankful we want justice and not revenge.

Sheela na Gig

Liz Darling

Sovereignty

H. Byron Ballard

The morning news was grim but not surprising. We were celebrating the summer solstice in a nature preserve that once was a strip mine. There is an open coal seam near the ritual circle, a constant reminder of what this land was and how it suffered, a suffering that ended only thirty years ago. It was saved from that life by good people with a vision and its regeneration is visual as well as visceral. To stand on this self-healing land in southern Ohio is to touch the possibility of renewal for the biosphere and all the beings that live within and upon it.

Connection to the outside world is blessedly sparse here so it felt significant that my phone pinged to wake me with the news that the US Supreme Court had removed physical sovereignty from over half the population of the nation. With an elaborate and carefully worded document, the decision that had been settled law for decades was overturned, leaving American women of child-bearing years without the ability to make decisions about their reproductive lives. Those decisions are now being made by state legislators—predominantly men—with little or no regard for the lives of women or the hard decisions many must make.

The news spread throughout the camp. Women gathered in small groups to weep, to curse, to hold their vulnerability in their bare hands for all of us to see. There was so much anger and unrelenting fury. The men at the gathering tried awkward comfort but soon stepped away. They and we were powerless in the face of so much wrath. The stones on the road felt it. The trees bowed towards it. The waters of the lake rippled with the unspoken howl of it.

We paced like caged beasts. We drank too early, lacing our coffee with rum and whisky. Our heads were covered in tangles of hair, our faces left unwashed and our teeth unbrushed as we ranted and cried. Not for the first time, we grieved the help that did not come, we spat on the elected officials who allowed such a thing to happen, and we were overcome with the shame and guilt of not working harder to prevent what we all knew was inevitable with the three judges appointed by a president bereft of honor, unknown to wisdom. We knew, and yet we hoped and wished and dreamed that those in power would see the danger to us, would act with speed, would do what we knew could be done though we ourselves could not do it. We needed this profound piece of our healthcare, a piece that had only been held in the hands of women for ages past, we needed them to make it the law of the land, inviolable. Year after year, administration after administration, campaign promise after broken promise, women waited for elected men to do the right and appropriate thing. Time after time, this was left undone in favor of spending political capital in ways deemed more important, more timely.

Now it was undone and so were we. We stumbled through this hollow land for hours until a trio of the event organizers came to me with a request. Would I consider holding some space that evening for people to talk, to grieve? I nodded. We'll be on the stage this evening, I responded. We will make ritual together.

The rest of the afternoon was spent gathering stones and working it through in my head. I made a few notes. I prayed and made offering to the Divines I serve, and to the spirits of this healing land. I sat in the stone circle and let that healing flow over and through me. My thoughts turned to the ancestral women who had needed this right and didn't have it—the women who died because they tried to prevent the birth of yet another child into a family that couldn't feed and tend the children already born. The women who ruined their health with quack remedies for a serious health problem. The women who died rather than give birth to a rapist's child.

A cold veil fell over me then. I could see those times upon us again. We need more than wishes and hopes now. We need to wield the power that is our birthright. We must be clear-eyed about the fact that no one is coming to "save" us. Women have always been expendable, our rights always a second thought, our success always in our own hands. My soul changed in those moments. The tender care and grieving were set aside then and my spirit was as clear and cold as a mountain stream, moving, digging in, flowing through. The Mothers had wrapped me in their cloak of authority and placed in my hands a staff.

My priestess-self went to the stage and set up a temple for the work of the evening. There wasn't a sense of how many would be present but that was immaterial. This work of ritualizing our spirits spread throughout the land there. I waited, not reviewing what we would do, only listening to the sounds of the trees and the stones, and the soft voices of my community going to supper, glancing at the stage.

So much in our lives is difficult and heart-shattering. Even the small things that present to us as inconveniences and annoyances bring with them opportunities to stand up, or postpone or ignore, shoving it away for another day. Bypassing the meaning and the lesson because there seems to be so little time to pick it apart and suck the juices from its hard shell.

Ceremony and ritual give us places to put all the sharp emotions that strike at us from our personal histories and from our daily lives. The workaday world allows for little rituals everywhere to mark the rite of passage or the ordinary work that polishes our souls and elevates our spirits. We find that marking such passages gives meaning as well as clarity to our work and to the next steps on the path for us.

That evening we stood in a ragged circle, ever widening as more and more people joined us. It is the way with circles and why that shape is ever with us Goddess-folk. All good-hearted people are welcomed in, invited in, and the circle ever expands to fit their number. It is easy to take hands in a circle, to put your arms around sad shoulders in a circle, to see each person and hold them in the beat of your heart.

We began as we often do by honoring the land around us, the directions, elements, Ancestors. We called in Absent Friends and our Foremothers. We breathed together. We listened to the birds as they settled for the night.

I spoke of our grief and anger. I reminded us all that we were not alone, that community is the woven basket that holds us and all we contain. We stepped one step toward the center—the heart—of the circle so that we stood shoulder to shoulder, supporting each other. Holding each other up.

We talked of sovereignty and what that means when you are not part of a royal family. The women there told stories of decisions made and promises kept, and how the experiences of claiming personal physical sovereignty made them stronger. There was some sadness, a little guilt but no shame.

Women in that circle stood a little straighter as they listened. Hugs were offered and accepted. There was even some awkward laughter. I don't remember much about the ritual, the ceremony. The energy was strong and grew stronger. I handed each of them a smooth stone that was gathered from the road in the afternoon: a stone for our strength, our will, our work, our connection to each other and this healing land. This land that heals us, each of us, as it heals itself.

We had a few more days together and there were many conversations about where we go, what we do now. How we remake the world and wield our power to do so. Connections were made that continue, so many months later. Months in which some in power have shown us that there are shining lights, and others have shown us the depth and breadth of our oldest enemy, this ancient misogyny.

What we have learned—again and perhaps finally—is that our bodies and souls are intertwined like a double helix and our power is revealed in these times of challenge and danger. These twists of self and spirit reach out to our farthest grandmothers and our most distant unknown descendants: a braid of wisdom made manifest in our physical and spiritual sovereignty. We are circles within circles, plaited and woven, strong, and resilient.

May we all remember well.

Iceberg

Liz Darling

The Greatest Lie

Arlene Bailey

Poked and probed
Assaulted and violated
They say my vagina
Belongs only to others
But Never to me

Nailed to the cross
Of male desire
I'm told to submit
And open wide
For my vagina
Belongs to others
But not to me

Cross your legs
And act like a lady
But Open your legs
And let me in
For I am male
And the arbiter
Of the code of
Decency for your
Inner regions

But know this,
That I have no
Responsibility for
Any child that may
Come from me
Taking my pleasure
When and how I please

That is your gift from
My god and your
Cross to bear
So hang on the cross
As others grab for your
Pussy and keep your legs
Crossed except for me
Don't allow yourself
Pleasure as that too
Is only for me

You know...

Man, The Male
The Dominant Human

AND

Arbiter of ALL things
Female

Roe Versus Wade

Philomena van Rijswijk

Down to the Bone

Mary Saracino

Bones don't lie.
Bodies don't either.
Women are tired, weary,
subjugated, colonized.
For thousands of years
our tongues have been silenced
our raging mouths sutured shut.
Every day we fight an endless war.
Rape—or the fear of it—plagues us,
walking on college campuses,
strolling down the street,
getting into or out of our cars,
taking the subway,
going shopping, washing clothes at the laundromat,
and a million other
ordinary activities that occupy our days.
There is violence everywhere,
from fists and guns,
laws and lovers,
bosses and priests,
politicians and judges
controlling our un-tame-able nature.
We know life is fragile, precarious, precious.
We sing, we dance,
we howl at the moon,
we bleed our monthly blood,
we birth the world's children,
tend to aging parents,
we counsel our grandchildren,
bury our dead.

We clean and cook,
cry and laugh,
pray and ponder.
We make art,
make love, make peace.
Still, every day we are erased
or discarded,
our essence invisible
to the unwilling eyes of
the powerful folks, the ordinary ones too,
that refuse to relinquish their stranglehold
on our self-determination
unless we cede our sovereignty to placate
their ideal version of womanhood
a mirage based on subterfuge.
We are so much more than lipstick,
makeup, frilly dresses, fancy hairdos, bling;
those are costumes,
they do not make us female,
they do not define our power.
Some of us cower,
others fight back
remembering a time long, long ago.
We refuse to swallow our truth,
deny our worth.
Our hearts are on fire,
our tongues are swollen with grief,
with desire
for justice
for equality.
We hunger for a deeper restitution
that honors our immeasurable, innate humanity,
returns to us ownership of our uteruses
our hearts, our minds.
We have been robbed of our stories,
our cultures, our spiritual traditions—every woman
of every race, color, creed, ethnicity.

We belong to the Earth, and she to us.
We belong to each other.
We must shout that from the depths of our lungs,
let it reverberate in the sea of our marrow.
We must always, ever, be vigilant, fierce
until we can, without flinching, proclaim—and own—
the truth of our lives
down to the bone
down to the bone
down to the bone.

Song from the Unwanted

Louise M Wisechild

I remember deciding not to have children when I was 8-years-old. I didn't want to inflict the misery of my childhood onto another captive child, even while I looked longingly into the windows of other kids and wished someone would hold me.

Nor did I want to grow up and become my impatient, cruel, impotent and burdened mother, who like most "good wives" of the 1950s, was expected to have children. Parenthood was not a calling or a joy or a passion. In the time before birth control pills and abortion, choice rarely entered into discussions. I was eighteen before Roe v. Wade became law and freed me from the fear of pregnancy.

There are many reasons the *Dobbs* decision filled me with rage, from the limited choices offered to my single mother in the 1950s, to my experience of incest and abuse in my family, to the singular amount of love and resources that I know good parenting requires.

And then there are the stories of my friend, an abortion doctor and the most compassionate woman I know. Her stories — fourteen-year-olds from troubled families; women with children already; women battered, threatened, abandoned; poor women; women with important dreams; failed birth control; women who said they didn't "believe" in abortion, but now they had a "real need, not like those others."

At the clinics where she worked, those who didn't "believe" in abortion screamed "murderer" and "baby killer" at her while shaking their posters of impossibly over-developed fetuses and Bible verses. But beyond "forced birth," the protestors did not fight to make life better for the mothers or the babies they believed they were saving. Rather, "forced birthing" separates the welfare of the baby from that of the mother, despite the fact that this bond of secure attachment allows a child to grow into successful human relationships.

For the unwanted among us, this human journey to feel connected can be much more challenging. These many years later, I know that my choice not to have children was best for me and for any child I might have had.

Song from the Unwanted is written from the perspective of the unwanted unborn.

https://on.soundcloud.com/c1BA

Song from the Unwanted
Louise Wisechild/Peter Bladh

I don't want to be your baby
If you don't want me
Cause I'd need you
Mornings through nights
I want a welcome
That you're ready to feel
Coz A baby should be wanted
To make it all right

I know you're stressed out
No money for rent
And the guy you slept with
Says "it" isn't his
You're working three jobs
At school till late at night
But a baby should be wanted
To grow up all right

vs 2
I don't want to be a burden
Or ruin your dreams
Or live with a longing
Where love's s'posed to be
I want good attention
So I can thrive
Cause a baby should be wanted
To grow up all right

I know you're young or
You've got other kids
Don't want to look like the rapist
Or your father who slipped in
Giving birth is fraught
And health care is a fight
And a baby should be wanted
To make it all right

vs.3
I don't want to be unwanted
And born in the States
There's no help for families
And the schools are not safe
I'd rather be in Norway
Where the parents get paid
Coz A baby should be wanted
To make it all right

It's your life, I want
A mama who's free
Whose got what she needs
And has enough for me
If you're not ready
Then now's not the time
Cuz a baby should be wanted
To grow up all right.

The State of her, Ireland's own
Dee Mulrooney

This piece is a reflection on what it means to be a woman and in particular an Irish woman. Lifting the skirt, a blessing or a curse depending on those gazing.

Why Understanding the Word "Mother" Is Vital to Women's Sovereignty and Body Autonomy in the Wake of Roe v. Wade

Sharon Smith

Mother = Mater = Matter

Matter, the substance of which all things are comprised, arises from the Latin word, *mater* —"origin, source, mother," according to Michiel de Vaan, whose work is considered the gold standard of etymological work in Latin, and Calvert Watkins, professor of linguistics at Harvard. We also get our English word, Mother, from the same root word. It's no surprise to me, as a devotee of the Great Cosmic Mother (i.e., the Goddess), that this should be so. I have come to see creation as a Divine Feminine, and *divinely feminine*, principle. As the Great Mother shapes matter into galaxies, stars, planets, and life forms upon those planets throughout the Cosmos, so, too, do females shape matter into life forms, many utilizing the Creative Cauldron of the Womb; thus, Matter and Mother dance the Spiral Dance of Creation together.

ALL mothers, whether human or animal upon this good Earth, are expressions of the Great Cosmic Mother – her physical portals of life through which souls enter and re-enter this physical reality.
Is it any wonder that the word "Mother" is one of the oldest words in any language?

However, what people have largely forgotten is that "Mother" once was understood, acknowledged, and honored not only as a Life-giver, but as the one who had the final say over life; i.e., *whether to give it or not*. No one questioned a Woman's right to terminate a pregnancy, because she had exclusive autonomy over her body and its Womb-Tomb. As that Sacred Portal of the Divine Feminine, she alone had the right to close the Gateway and not permit a soul to enter it, or enter into the world through it.

But under Patriarchy, that Divine Right of Woman was branded as evil and taken by force from her. Women were then subjugated to men under their "Father God" religions, forced to submit to the will and the laws of men, and essentially made the property of men. And they were taught that abortion was a great evil — how can man amass his "quiver full of children," if Women are allowed to stop the process from unfolding? A Woman who aborts, they said, is a terrible person and must be punished. Unfortunately, centuries of patriarchal oppression find Women today still buying into it, believing it...

And here we are today, 2023, a supposed Enlightened Age for humanity... and the Patriarchs are at it again, using the hammer of religion and the anvil of politics to break the Sovereignty and Bodily Autonomy of Women that we have fought so long and hard to reclaim.

The overturning of Roe v. Wade, championed by fundamentalist Evangelical Christianity and carried out by conservative Republican politics, is not so much about abortion as it is about Patriarchy's inability to understand the polarity (the state of having two opposite aspects) of the Feminine—the power of Life and Death. Men have always feared that power because they cannot birth life into being; they can only take and destroy life. But Women have the power to do both.

Because of the suppression and blatant maligning of this ancient Divine Feminine Truth, humanity has forgotten that Mother was NOT originally just a "Life-Giver" and "Nurturer," as we have come to believe... but also "She Who Shuts the Gateway of Life"... Because we were created to keep and hold the Balance between Life and Death.

Nature always seeks a Balance. And it is the Feminine (in humanity, the Woman) who has been called to keep it – NOT the masculine (the man).

Man has made a grievous error in trespassing upon this Sacred Ground, and we must not sit by and allow it to continue. It's time to rise up in our Divine Feminine rage, reclaim and re-establish the full and sacred meaning of "Mother."

Wet Spring

Liz Darling

Take your Prayers, Hear my Words

Manya Kapikian

Take your prayers
Hear my words
I am cursed
I do not believe
in your god
in your divine

I am free
because I believe
dual in nature
sprung from one
Goddess of light & dark
divinity be

Fallen angels
poised in living form
removed the womb and
bound in tyrannical chains

Hear my words
above the darkest lake
I reach beyond my reflection
into the depths of your shadow

I am cursed
by your righteous bible verse
thoughts & prayers
for my eternal salvation
glory your praise in elevation

I say to you
to those who prey
by words that do not bind me
by laws that do not represent me

My blood is not yours to take
I left that Garden awake
I am a sovereign being in body form
The Choice is mine.
free will is my divine

I return to you this which is true
I own what is mine
and return what you seek.

Human Body

Rachael Noton

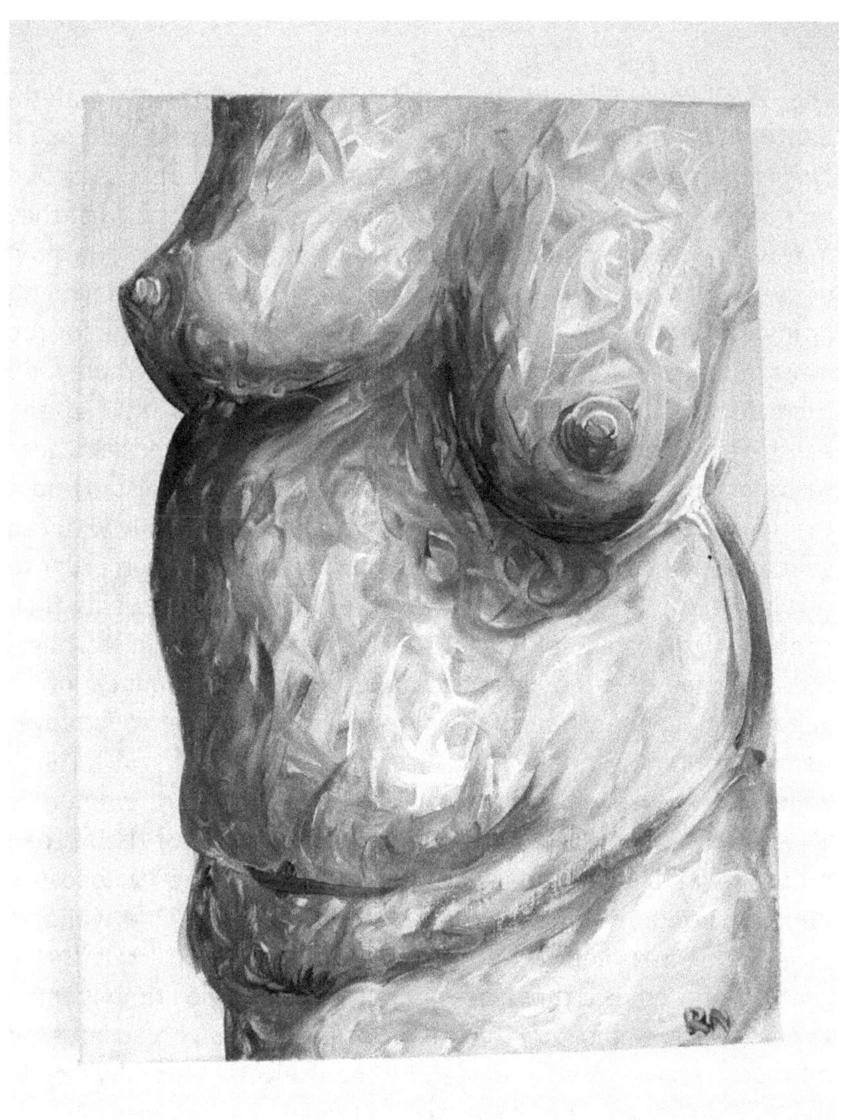

The Panoptic Monotheocratic Eye Appropriating Women's Bodies[3]

Gillian M.E. Alban

The "well-known study 'Iran and Gilead: Two Late-Twentieth-Century Monotheocracies'" referenced in The Historical Notes on *The Handmaid's Tale* by Margaret Atwood (372) discusses two monotheistic religions taking control of women's bodies; what they may wear, what they may do or say, whether they may be educated or even literate, whether they may gain remunerative employment, or instead whether they may be rented out without charge for the most intimate of relations, to be a species of breeding whore, and then discarded, thus how the identity of women is defined and controlled in terms of their sex and their breeding potential. These restraints approximate the position of women in Afghanistan under the Taliban, where if you don't have a man in your family who can gain a paying job, you might need to disguise as a man in order to survive, as in *The Breadwinner* by Deborah Ellis. In twenty-first-century Afghanistan, it is legal to sell a six-year-old girl in marriage, but a woman does not possess the legal right to an education or gainful employment, and for any public activity, she must cover herself entirely in opaque cloth, except for a small grill through which she may peer. Such cultures apparently regard women as Middle Ages plague victims, ringing a bell to notify of their dread presence, watching church services from a crack in the wall because for them to join the healthy is deemed hazardous. One wonders how God is assumed to have made women so monstrous that a glimpse of them is a threat to men, or what terrible crime women appear accountable for, that their visible presence causes such outrage amongst men, who assume themselves created by God in the divine image. The Bible, translated at a time when 'man' referred to both sexes, states: "So God created man in his/her own

---

[3] I would like to dedicate this chapter to the following wonderful women: Gonca and Bilge Alban, Simge Eren, Zoe Tillyard, Vicki Wallbank and Lizzie Kew; all power to them!

image, in the image of God created he them; male and female created he them:" (Genesis 1, 27). From this text Joseph Campbell logically infers that "God is himself the original androgyne" (Campbell 54) in creating both sexes in the image of himself, and any attempt to assume he or she has masculine shape is entirely mistaken. The newly literate Becka in Atwood's *The Testaments* gains this insight while reading the Bible as an Aunt in Gilead, learning that "we're in God's image, male and female both" (*Testaments* 295), protesting that they leave those parts out.

This chapter reflects on both the real and imaginative or literary status of women in monotheocracies, taking its major examples from Iran and a fictional America in the twentieth century, after a ruthless revolution has destroyed human rights in both countries, but especially those of women. To these examples I add a third example from a novel set in Canaan at the birth of these monotheisms thousands of years ago, recreating life under emerging Judaism. The American example of Gilead is a fictional extrapolation of tendencies in fanatically religious societies, demonstrating how women's rights must be re-won in each generation, and how sex and reproduction may fall under state control, also seen in George Orwell's *Nineteen Eighty-Four*.

However extreme the examples presented here, the objectification of woman and her body held under the male gaze, assuming rights over any child she may bear, indicates the presumed worthlessness of half the human race, the life givers. Tomalin shows Jane Austen's contemporaries asking each other if they have finished breeding or not, also describing men returning home at night and removing children from their bed in order to enjoy their own conjugal rights, regardless of how many more children their wives may be capable of bearing and surviving. Today we observe female rights as under threat in Islamic states, yet we have recently learned that rights won in the so-called civilized western world are also precarious and liable to be rescinded without redress. The Supreme Court of the United States has overruled women's right to abortion "on the grounds that the substantive right to abortion was not 'deeply rooted in this Nation's history or tradition" and only gained in the *Roe* case of 1973, thereby making any legal or social progress impossible (*Roe v. Wade*).

A woman's right to her own body and any child she may or may not determine to bear, remains precarious in many places. Helen Lewis quotes Katha Pollitt reminding us that beneath our assumptions regarding women's rights to "vote and go to college and have a family and a job [...] is the secret underground life of women [through which women will always be blamed for whatever they attempt], because the real reason you are here on earth is to produce children, and you shirk that duty at your peril'" (in Lewis, 283). Lewis reminds us that "the more the foetus is treated as a person, the less its mother is" (285). Countering the pro-lifers, she enquires how it is possible for a state to overrule a woman's bodily autonomy, regarding either her womb or her kidney. She cites the grave case of the thirty-one-year-old Savita Halappanavar living in Galway in 2012. When Savita started miscarrying, she reached Galway Hospital with the foetus "protruding from her uterus into her vagina" (292), only to be refused an abortion, leading to her developing sepsis. Despite eventually managing to deliver the foetus before an abortion drug could be administered, she died within four days, in a case which was declared "tantamount to murder" (292). Crystal in *The Testaments* is similarly slaughtered; cut open to enable the birth of baby Mark, she is regarded as having made the ultimate sacrifice, however she never consented to this murder (*Testaments* 103-5). Savita's case in Ireland became instrumental in the repeal of the notorious Eighth Amendment which had assigned equal weight to the lives of both mother and foetus, preventing pregnant women from receiving proper care (Lewis 291), with a two-thirds majority finally agreeing on the "woman's right to choose whether or not to have an abortion" (300). However, in the same year of 2018, Donald Trump's first act was to reinstate the 'global gag 'of barring NGOs from receiving government funding if they mention abortion. By filling the Supreme Court with conservatives, "*Roe v. Wade*, the legislation which gave women 'existential freedom, 'was [placed] in jeopardy"

(298), with the resulting truncation of women's rights that has now been enshrined in law in America. Not without reason Atwood wrote in defense of *The Handmaid's Tale*: "if you see a person heading toward a large hole in the ground, is it not a friendly act to warn him?" She states that nothing she writes is without precedent (*In Other Worlds* 244).

Handmaids Under the Eyes

In Atwood's nightmare dystopian theocracy related in *The Handmaid's Tale* and *The Testaments*, the government of Gilead mercilessly inflicts its own system after the revolution, shooting the president, machine-gunning Congress and declaring a state of emergency: "the police, or the army, or whoever they were, would open fire almost as soon as any of the marches even started" (*Handmaid's* 226), thus crushing any opposition, with wars continuing against opposed foreign forces. The attack that liquidated Congress is blamed on Islamic terrorists, while the Constitution is suspended under a state of emergency (*Testaments* 66-67). Women doctors and lawyers are rounded up and brutally reconditioned in stadiums; those who are not shot are hardened into advocates of the regime to build "a society congruent with the Divine order" (174) which read congruent with the lascivious desires of power-hungry men, seizing the progenitive and other labour of women; *Per Ardua Cum Estrum* (33), and separating male and female spheres. Enemies of the regime, including "'gender traitors,' nonwhite races, religious minorities, and especially women" (Wilson 275) are hooked up on the Wall under white and bloody hoods after Particicution or execution by lynching in order to root out all opposition. The Handmaid protagonist understands her situation when her computer ID number is challenged as invalid, preventing her from buying cigarettes; she is simultaneously released or "let go" from work (*Handmaid's* 221). Women are deleted in one electronic stroke as "F" under a new law stealing their identity; deprived of employment, their social identity as reasonable beings is deemed redundant, and their resources are handed over to a male relative or stolen by the state, reducing them to minors under the guardianship of male relatives or forcing them underground (224).

Women are required to cover their bodies at all times, with fertile women also using white wings like horse blinkers, making it almost impossible for them to see or to be seen. They are rounded up as resources under pretexts such as being in an illegal relationship, defined as either partner having been divorced, with this fundamentalist regime pronouncing marriage indissoluble, even retrospectively. They are then placed in Rachel and Leah Re-education or Red Centers to be indoctrinated, after which they are rented out or enslaved without any means of escape. A practice recorded thousands of years ago in the Bible is reinstated, by which the mothers of the tribes of Israel, when unable to bear children themselves, ask their husband to "go in unto" their handmaid, often a half-sister from another mother who has not had a dowry paid to her father. All these women are chattel, but some have a price and legal status, while others are rented out as handmaids within the marriage of their owners. At this dawn of civilization, wives in polygamous relationships become mothers of their children, while handmaids remain slaves, lacking legal rights over their body or its offspring.

The major Ceremony of the dystopian society of Gilead occurs with the rented woman lying between the man and his wife in bed, as he proceeds to fuck the handmaid (the narrator suggests a few alternate words here, including copulate, which involves two people, and rape, indicating force, which is not used, although there was not much choice; 116). The rented woman is appropriated to enable the barren wife to be fruitful and multiply, bearing the child she is unable to have herself. The three form a monstrous, multiple-bodied creature on the bed, the slave adjunct trapped in the middle, without control over her body, as she attempts to conceive a child which will be stolen from her even in the act of giving birth. She becomes a "two-legged womb," a "sacred vessel," or an "ambulatory chalice" (*Handmaid's* 171) through such appropriation or "genital rental" (in Wilson 276).

These women's bodies are thus used to create surrogate offspring for the infertile leaders of the religious dictatorship.

This nightmare scenario uses the *Old Testament* precedent of Rachel, who, despairing of having her own child, directs her husband Jacob to sexually use her handmaid Bilhal to bear the child that God has not given her. Rachel is not the first to use this expedient; her grandmother Sarai told Abram to "go in unto" her handmaid Hagar when she could not bear a child. Hagar ran away from Sarai's bad treatment, but returns when promised that her son Ishmael will become the father of multitudes. Sarai herself then conceives in her old age and has Isaac, with whom God makes his covenant, including male circumcision. Isaac has one wife Rebecca, strikingly following the precept of leaving mother and father to become one flesh in monogamous marriage. The two wives of Jacob with their handmaids become the mothers of the sons to become the twelve fathers of the tribes of Israel, thus placing this polygamous, handmaid situation at the core of Judaism.

Atwood shows the farcical situation of the wife and handmaid, almost totally clothed, for such societies always claim a hypocritical morality, lying on the bed together, with the commander tackling the lower trunk of the rented woman possessed of viable ovaries, as the wife sadistically crushes her rings into the slave's hands, then after the ceremony ordering her out, the procreative juices running down her legs. Indoctrinated into the necessity of bearing a child for her owners, indeed without choice, any handmaid who conceives the desired child in this warped scenario will undergo pregnancy and a painful, natural birth, only for the baby to be stolen from her and placed in the arms of the sterile wife, who will name the child and bring it up. The handmaid thus 'rents-a-womb' for nine months plus breastfeeding, then, bereft of her child, she is turned out of the house and relentlessly moved on to her next posting, where she will attempt to have another baby, who will be similarly stolen from her. For this essential service, these scapegoat handmaids, referred to as sluts, are debasingly assumed to need redemption "through the sacrifice of their bodies and their [procreative] labour" (*Testaments* 33). Meanwhile, Dr. Grove in *loco parentis* rapes his four-year-old child Becka, and paedophile Bluebeard Commander Judd salivates over a prospective new young wife, Nicole.

Anita Diamant's *The Red Tent* is narrated by Dinah, the only daughter amongst the twelve sons of Jacob of Israel, offering a view of this system in ancient Canaan and Haran. The mothers enter a bigamous marriage, as the beautiful Rachel is retained by her father Laban, who first tricks Jacob into marriage with the older sister Leah. Diamant's sympathetic recreation tells of a fourteen-year-old Leah supervising the herdsman duties with flocks of sheep and goats, trading wool with Aleppo, managing the stores, tents and cooking; as Laban is a lazy, useless father, Leah takes charge of the entire settlement in all but name. Jacob engages in a practical relationship with her regarding their working lives, during which they are observed circling each other like "rutting he-goats" (34), causing Leah to desire this man engaged to her younger sister for her beauty, while Jacob relieves himself in the fields dreaming of both sisters. Leah's handmaid, noting this situation, fills the young Rachel, scarcely menstruating at twelve, with fearful accounts regarding the freakish size of Jacob's sex, culminating in Rachel panicking and declaring her unreadiness for marriage and yielding her place to Leah. After the wedding the couple consummate and enjoy a week of honeymoon rights, when Jacob emerges from his tent in feigned anger to assert that Laban tricked him with the older girl and demanding marriage to the lovely Rachel, asking for the sisters Zilpah as Leah's dowry and Bilhah as Rachel's dowry, confirming their handmaid status as breeding slaves, without rights over their own lives in these polygamous marriages (41).

As Leah bears many sons, Rachel frequently miscarries, until her handmaid Bilhah offers to go in to Jacob on her behalf, to "bear a son on your knees. Let me be your womb and your breasts. Let me bleed your blood and shed your tears. Let me become your vessel until your time comes" (60), as Bilhah goes to Jacob's tent one night as a maid, to emerge without bridal status. Subsequently they share the birthing stool and "womb for the awful hour when the baby pushed his way out [...] as though a two-headed woman had given birth" (64-65).

Despite the affection between these two half-sisters, this results in a strained relationship over both husband and the child who is legally Rachel's while biologically Bilhah's. Rachel does subsequently bear Joseph herself in a breech birth continuing through days of agony, enabling the beautiful Rachel to partake in the sorority and vindication of motherhood then prized. She later perishes in agony and black blood, giving birth to her second son on the road, whom she names Ben-Oni, son of her woe (248), although Jacob overrules her last wish by calling him Benjamin. Rachel also works as a midwife, gleaning these essential skills from the midwife Inna. The concept of stay-at-home women is a nineteenth-century middle-class myth; women have always worked harder than men and been remunerated less for it, still performing "nearly two-thirds of all working hours [to receive] only one-tenth of the world income and [to] own less than 1 percent of world property" (Wolf 23).

Diamant suggests a love relationship between Dinah and Shalem of the city of Shechem, which is recorded in Genesis as rape; however, Shalem not only offers Dinah's brothers a superb dowry, but also complies with their request to become circumcised, along with all the city's men. This enables Dinah's brothers to descend on and wipe out the entire male population, resulting in the slaughter of Shechem, as Dinah, waking up covered in blood, returns to her family to resoundingly curse them before deserting them. She calls out to Jacob: "Jacob, your sons have done murder.[...] Jacob shall never know peace again.[...] Jacob knows my words are true. Look at me, for I wear the blood of the righteous men of Shechem. Their blood stains your hands and your head, and you will never be clean again" (Diamant 245-46). Widowed and pregnant, Dinah journeys with her similarly bereaved mother-in-law to Egypt. Campbell informs us how sociological mythologies assert morality within a bounded field, assuming moral rules to be applicable only within one's own community, but not considering them binding to those outside the tribe, the out-group, thereby enabling such savage *Old Testament* massacres (Campbell 22); Jacob thus earns the title of butcher of Shechem. Dinah, like her aunt-mother Rachel, is a midwife and briefly a beloved wife, subsequently bearing a son in Egypt who calls her Ma, but she remains his barbarian nurse mother, as the boy's grandmother assures her that it is she who is the official mother of the child and hence able to determine his name and upbringing, thus indicating a species of handmaiding in the more developed society of Egypt. Dinah enjoys nine years at home with her son, with their relations becoming more formal, until he leaves home for his education and she virtually loses him.

Partial Female Communities

The mother of Atwood's narrator had desired a female culture (*Handmaid's* 159), living as a wild, independent Artemis, birthing her desired daughter at the age of thirty-seven, and not bothering to retain the father, since she saw a man as "just a woman's strategy for making other women" (151). At this time women had power over their own bodies in relationships, maternity and work. Her daughter Offred constitutes a throwback whose mother's activism during the porn riots and abortion riots embarrasses her. Atwood thus illustrates how the pendulum may swing from radicalism to regression, the daughter emerging tamer than her radical mother, who "expected too much from me, [...] to vindicate her life for her, and the choices she'd made" (153). "No mother is ever, completely, a child's idea of what a mother should be, and I suppose it works the other way around as well" (227). She finally appreciates her mother's attempts to bring her up according to her forceful ideas, while remaining oblivious to her own eroding freedoms. Her mother had been a virulent protester, actively engaged in marches for women's rights and defending the "FREEDOM TO CHOOSE. EVERY BABY A WANTED BABY. RECAPTURE OUR BODIES. DO YOU BELIEVE A WOMAN'S PLACE IS ON THE KITCHEN TABLE?" protesting the back-street abortions women had resorted to in the previous era (150), as legal abortion became unavailable. Offred only appreciates her mother when it is too late, glimpsing her on film cleaning up toxic waste in the colonies and leaving her mourning her loss.

Atwood's novels explore what could happen to women with a plummeting birth rate through chemical and nuclear pollution and the use of insecticides and herbicides, with children born deformed as a result of the poisoning of the ecosystem. But this is not our current situation; rather our planet Gaia, Mother Earth, cries out for help, overburdened with a human population and its constructions and waste far in excess of what can be viably sustained, placing all other life forms under threat of extinction, exhausting nature and water sources. Atwood shows the brutal dictatorship of Gilead obliterating independent thought or any alternate life, with the system justifying itself as an improvement on the previous one, shown as sexually aggressive against women, a frequent excuse of oppressive systems, which presents freedom **from** as more significant than the freedom **to do** anything. The narrator is left without agency over her life and held under panoptic vigilance. "Under His Eye" is a physical more than a symbolic threat, with patrolling Eyes omnipresent. Wilson categorizes the wife Serena as a sterile Madonna, Offred as a fallen Mary Magdalene, and her rebellious friend Moira(i) exemplifying Fate as a Jezebel, forming a trinity of goddesses or archetypal women (277, 283). Offred also represents a grieving Madonna or Demeter, longing for her lost child, with Serena and the authoritative Aunts as Athenas, aligned with the theocratic rulers of this system; Moira is a self-assertive woman attempting to determine her own destiny under cruel oppression.

The previous inhabitant of Offred's room hanged herself before being captured, after scratching in the cupboard: "*Nolite te bastardes carborundorum*" (*Handmaid's* 65), decoded by the commander as: "Don't let the bastards grind you down." He is compared to brutal Nazi leaders who assume a human face outside their savage duties of destroying the helpless. After their first forbidden date, involving word games rather than sex play, the narrator bursts into the uncontrollable seismic mirth rhyming with birth (183), the defiant laughter that Cixous describes in "The Laugh of Medusa." She is found on the floor the next morning by the Martha servant, confronted with an apparent suicide attempt similar to that made by the previous handmaid. As Carter asserts in *The Sadeian Woman*, and as is crystal clear in any society that pays lip service to the honour of mothers, the glorification of the maternal function, far from doing anything for women, merely enslaves them within compulsory maternity, disempowering them in their very ability to bear children. Visiting a hotel of Jezebels with the Commander, Offred finds the rebellious Moira there, after her failed escape attempts and much torture, confined to a Jezebel's life. For the powerful, nothing has changed; they do not follow the puritan morality they inflict on their helpless followers. The lesbian Moira reports that these sex workers are frequently lesbian, affording men scant value in this warped and twisted society.

Offred's most haunting dreams are of running to embrace her precious daughter, for her only to be inexorably snatched away, leaving mother and daughter stretching their arms out helplessly towards each other. Such dreams of her daughter are her worst experience, leaving her waking disoriented and distraught (*Handmaid's* 93). Seeing a photo of her stolen, lost daughter is unbearable for her: "She's in good hands,' they said. 'With people who are fit. You are unfit, but you want the best for her. Don't you?" (49). They have erased her from her daughter's consciousness, telling her that her mother is dead.

Diamant in *The Red Tent* shows fertile women managing to create a periodic female sanctuary within the rhythm of their cycles, also suggesting the Haran family of Laban worshipping goddesses, until Jacob asserts the monotheistic worship of El, the God who is not shown in images. As "the god of thunder, high places and awful sacrifice," he could require a father to cast out his son "or slaughter him outright" (15). The mother Adah has to defend her daughters from their lecherous father Laban; she beats him until she draws blood and threatens to curse him until he brings home gold bangles and a beautiful Asherah pillar in compensation; the women place this idol on the bamah or high place to sacrifice to her (24). For these women, a girl's first menses is cause of rejoicing, as they massage her, feed her honey-date cakes in the triangular shape of the vulva, give her wine, and marry her to the earth by easing her onto the Asherah pillar while calling on Inanna, Queen of the Night, to accept her blood so that in her blood she would give life (206). The Canaanite women are shocked at such 'abominations,' instead adopting the patriarchal display of bloody sheets from the bridal tent as proof of a bride's virginity (207), turning their maidenhood into a male prize (197). Rachel as a midwife gains status as the servant of Eknath the healer (57); she steals the teraphim or family gods and goddesses from Laban; when Laban enters the red tent for them, she defies him to take them from beneath her. The wives value and celebrate Dinah's birth as a beloved daughter, one to whom they could relate their stories and who would carry their traditions into the next generation; they particularly bless her against the baby-stealer, Lamashtu (81).

The strikingly redheaded Werenro invites them to the barley festival, a precedent of the later Demeter Mysteries, celebrated in the sacred grove of Rebecca the grandmother at Mamre. Jacob tells Esau that Sarai the wife of Abram was a servant of Inanna, daughter of Nanna and Ningal, who awarded her a son late in life (162). Rebecca recounts her grief at losing many children through miscarriage (182), despite which Isaac does not replace her with handmaids. Dinah meets her cousin Tabea, who wishes to serve as a consecrated woman at the altar of a temple such as in Shechem, where she will sleep alone, unless taking a consort at the barley festival, while Dinah the midwife declares herself fearless of childbirth. But Rebecca rejects Tabea and her mother, since she has left the women's ways by isolating her daughter during her first menses rather than celebrating them in the red tent. Leah explains this as Rebecca's disappointment at the loss of the mothers' ways and the "great mother," who goes by many names, but who is in danger of being forgotten" (186). She informs Dinah that Inanna is a "fierce warrior and Death's bridesmaid. The great mother,

[Inanna] is the center of pleasure, the one who makes women and men turn to one another in the night [...] the queen of the ocean and the patron of the rain" (187). Inanna gives women the blood that flows "at the dark of the moon, the healing blood of the moon's birth" (187). However, Esau's family, the daughters of Esom, have abandoned the Opening and instead allow men to display dirty sheets "as though even the pettiest baal would require such a degradation in tribute" (188).

The red tent affords the women a place of female communion and restoration, with women celebrating and affirming their fallow periods together. Dinah anticipates idling with her mothers and sisters "in the ruddy shade of the red tent for three days and three nights, until first sight of the crescent goddess, [as her] blood will flow into the fresh straw, filling the air with the salt smell of women" (203). However, the women from other communities betray them, informing of their sacrifice during the first menses, as Jacob calls Rachel to account and destroys the teraphim, thus dividing their community. Dinah later encounters the apparently slaughtered Werenro surviving as a sistrum-player in Egypt; she has been raped and blinded, her face and body torn apart and left for dead by the road, possibly because of her striking red hair, or for her defiance in refusing to cry (303). Nafisi describes a woman who is arrested in Iran on a "trumped-up immorality charge" who is passed between the guards and repeatedly raped for the crime of her "amazing beauty;" they "married the virgins off to the guards, who would later execute them" (212), with men first enjoying beautiful women, and then blaming them and destroying them for their beauty which men find irresistible, leaving them helpless. As Nicole lands in Gilead from Canada, she can only sense "eyes, eyes, eyes, all over me like hands. I'd never felt so much at risk in that way— not even under the bridge with Gareth, and with strangers all around" (*Testaments* 272). Thus, we learn the imaginary crime of which women are accounted guilty. They are falsely blamed by guilty, lascivious men for their own wicked weakness, consuming and defacing women with their desecrating eyes and bodies.

The Female Body as Incendiary Device

The Iranian revolution of 1979 exerted endless restraints over women's lives, creating an unbalanced, unequal society of repressive bigotry and misogyny. Azar Nafisi in *Reading Lolita in Tehran* creates a memoir of her life in Iran after the revolution, discussing literature with her students after resigning her university post. Iranian women have not lost the right to education and professional work; however, the Islamic State exerts force over a woman's body by attempting to make it invisible, which ironically elevates it into a dangerous device, even as women are required to cover themselves in anonymity behind the veil. They are penalized for running up the stairs, laughing, for using or carrying makeup, and for talking to members of the opposite sex (9). The university pays scant attention to academic standards, but is obsessed with "the color of one's lips, the subversive potential of a single strand of hair" (11). Small acts like showing a strand of hair or growing nails, falling in love, holding hands or listening to music, become rebellious acts. The pious are not exempt, as a girl is jailed for five years for her affiliation to a dissident religious organization and banned from education for two more years; all deviations from the ratified sect of Islam are persecuted. Nafisi's pious grandmother resents the way the veil, to her "a symbol of her sacred relationship to God, had now become an instrument of power, turning the women who wore it into political signs and symbols" (103). Everything, including justice, is sacrificed to religious ideology, with the Blood of God teams patrolling the streets to ensure that the rules are applied, under posters declaring that "MEN WHO WEAR TIES ARE U.S. LACKEYS. VEILING IS A WOMAN'S PROTECTION [...] MY SISTER, GUARD YOUR VEIL. MY BROTHER, GUARD YOUR EYES" (27); a look passing between the sexes is found incendiary. Muslim girls are assumed modest virgins, keeping themselves for their husband; however, a pious uncle is free to tutor his eleven-year-old niece while sexually abusing her. Declaring that he is "keep[ing] himself chaste and pure for his future wife," three times a week he teaches her while his hands constantly "wandered over her legs, her whole body as he repeated the Arabic tenses" (48). The age of marriage is lowered from eighteen to nine, and stoning becomes "the punishment for adultery and prostitution" (27). Transgressing women are "hurled into patrol cars, taken to jail, flogged, fined, forced to wash the toilets and humiliated, and as soon as they leave, they go back and [courageously] do the same thing" (27). When obliged to veil herself, Nafisi decides to try and make her shamed body invisible, fleshless and boneless, until wishing to defy an "obstructionist figure of authority [she] would leave a few strands of hair out and make [her] eyes reappear, to stare at them uncomfortably" (168).

Women protest that "having children is their destiny as if they are doomed" (38). Her independent students become resentful of men, whom they find lacking equality with them, since this regime forces women to grow and mature, while the men around them "have not bothered to think" (38). Men are not exempt from the rules, including growing a beard, not shaking hands with members of the opposite sex (the plague victim again), clapping or whistling in meetings (25). But the sexual imbalance created is seen as a younger, spoiled brother can make his sister's life a misery while he attempts to prove "his masculinity by spying on her, listening to her telephone conversations, driving her car around and monitoring her actions" (16). Emily Brontë is condemned for appearing "to condone adultery" in *Wuthering Heights* (11), yet reading *Madame Bovary* and *Anna Karenina*, the students conclude "that an adulterous woman is much better than a hypocritical one" (51).

Nafisi describes a family of which the women are the powerful backbone. Dependable, hard-working at home and outside, they are mostly in arranged marriages to older "spoiled, nagging husbands, inferior to them intellectually and in every other way" (62). Of the uncles, one is killed by the Islamic Republic, while the rest have escaped to Europe or America. It is these uncles who comprise the hopes and dreams of the family, the fantasized Peter Pans who occasionally descend from their never-never land abroad to spread their enchantment.

Nafisi wonders at the dangerous power women have gained through actions like walking, talking, exposing a strand of hair, so devastating to the patrols, with men unable to control their feelings for women, shown by Cournut as men's trepidations before women in *Pourquoi les hommes ont peur des femmes*. Men enter the university freely, while women are taken through a curtained entrance to check their appearance and "level of attractiveness" (29); ostensibly aimed at creating female invisibility, such attentions rather make them "objects of curiosity" (30). Noting the power of a woman's hair to sexually provoke a man, her students wonder about "genitally mutilating men [...] so as to curb their sexual appetites" (70), as they read Nawal El Saadawi on the sexual mutilation of girls to curb their sexual desires, also related in Alice Walker's *Possessing the Secret of Joy*. The revolution claims men's sexual needs as a right; the Ayatollah writes about a man curing his sexual appetite by having sex with an animal. This creates the problem of chickens; after sex with a chicken, you may not eat it, but to what degree of proximity might a neighbour be allowed to eat that chicken? (71). Atwood relates such predatory desires: "The urges of men are terrible things and those urges need to be curbed. The man's eyes that were always roaming here and there like the eyes of tigers, those searchlight eyes, needed to be shielded from the alluring and indeed blinding power of "young women" (*Testaments* 9), whom men dare to castigate as "a source of temptation and evil" to themselves (Manji 154).

Nafisi's memoir indicates how brutality and banality come to overlap, in a false world based on a pernicious ideology, with saviour and executioner indistinguishable (23), the society exonerating itself by blaming its victims as Others, as Baudelaire states: "Hypocrite lecteur,—mon semblable,—mon frère" (44); the Other who is blamed for their own faults, as I discuss in *The Medusa Gaze*. Setting fire to cinemas, the state declares themselves not against cinema, but against prostitution; a blind film censor truncates any visible or imaginable artistic possibilities (24). Such societies use women as scapegoats to cover their weaknesses, seeing their own monstrosity mirrored back to them in those they presume to Other. She finds curiosity a necessity in order to maintain insubordination, yet under such an oppressive regime, children wake in terror at having illegal dreams (46). It is better for citizens of a totalitarian state not to dream, but internalized fears return at night to haunt them for any infringements they may or may not dare by day (46). After the continued slaughter of intellectuals and the violent transgression and truncation of any alternate lifestyle under state-sanctioned sexual molestation, she finally determines to abandon her homeland. The recent brutal murder of Mahsa Amini for exposing some of her hair simply confirms such disgust with this outrageous regime.

Pernicious panoptic control of the female body merely exposes male weakness and insecurity before a woman's appearance, as men, mastered by their own lascivious desires, fantasize women's flesh and desecrate it as the Other they are incapable of understanding. Presuming their own righteousness, men shamefully deface the purity of these Others. The pernicious, monotheocratic abuse of women and their bodies destroys the brimming bowls of women's free and independent lives, whether in enforced, enslaving maternity or in female sexual debasement. A woman is a human being, she is not a baby-producing machine.

Sources

Alban, Gillian M.E. *The Medusa Gaze in Contemporary Women's Fiction*. Newcastle-upon-Tyne: Cambridge Scholars Publishing, 2017.

Atwood, Margaret. *The Handmaid's Tale*. USA: Seal Books, Random House, 1985.

———. *The Testaments*. London: Chatto & Windus, 2019.

———. *In Other Worlds: SF and the Human Imagination*. Great Britain: Virago Press, 2011.

Cixous, Hélène. "The Laugh of the Medusa," *Signs*. The University of Chicago Press, 1/4, 1976, 875-93.

Carter, Angela. *The Sadeian Woman: An Exercise in Cultural History*. London: Virago Press, 1979.

Campbell, Joseph, with Bill Moyers. *The Power of Myth*. New York: Doubleday, 1988.

Cournut, Jean. *Pourquoi les hommes ont peur des femmes*. Paris: Presses Universitaires de France, 2001.

Dexter, Miriam Robbins. *Whence the Goddesses: A Source Book*. New York: Teachers College Press, 1990.

Diamant, Anita. *The Red Tent*. London: St. Martin's Press, 1997.

Ellis, Deborah. *The Breadwinner*. Oxford: Oxford University Press, 2000.

El Saadawi, Nawal. *Woman at Point Zero*. London: Zed, 2001.

The Holy Bible. London: Cambridge University Press, 1611.

Lewis, Helen. *Difficult Women: A History of Feminism in 11 Fights*. London: Jonathan Cape, 2020.

Nafisi, Azar. *Reading Lolita in Tehran: A Memoir in Books*. London: Harper Collins, 2003.

Manji, Irshad. *The Trouble with Islam Today: A Wake-up Call for Honesty and Change*. Toronto: Vintage Canada, 2003, 2005.

Patai, Raphael. *The Hebrew Goddess*. Detroit: Wayne State University Press, 1967, 1990.

Roe v. Wade, Wikipedia, 2022.

Tomalin, Claire. *Jane Austen: A Life*. London: Penguin Books, 1998, 2000.

Walker, Alice. *Possessing the Secret of Joy*. New York: Harcourt Brace, 1992.

Wilson, Sharon Rose. *Margaret Atwood's Fairy Tale Sexual Politics*. Toronto: University Press of Mississippi, 1993.

Wolf, Naomi. *The Beauty Myth*. London: Vintage Books, 1990.

Your Voice is Powerful
Claire Dorey

Keep Out of Our Caves

Conversations with Women, Reframed as Prose,
in Response to the Fall of Roe

Claire Dorey

I'll tell you why we women swim away from shore to the place where the cold grey sky meets the still grey sea. On misty mornings you may see us float over the horizon, where the light is silver and the edges are blurred. Sea of glass, swimming for sanity, each stroke and breath taking us away from the burden of being female, from the madness of what is happening back there on land. Ocean floor slipping away beneath our toes, we sprout our fishtails and set our sights on that distant rock where we lay our heads on empty miles and join a diaspora of mermaids whose rights drifted here on an insidious tide.

On that rock, we sigh our sighs and mourn the passing of First Wave pioneers, longing for the warmth of Second Wave arms, understanding the Third Wave is here. It's happening now. Women stuck back there on that fractious slither of land are drowning in a sludge of vindictiveness – patriarchal payback for Second and First Wave victories.

Energy centres activated, de-noised and de-cluttered from patriarchal conditioning, we must decide if we remain in the ocean, where the edges are soft, or return to land, where life has been made so very sharp and hard for us. If we return we come as Kitchen Table Rebels. We come with demands. The fall of Roe has left us speechless, so now we talk Non-Violent Direct Language, lobbying in solidarity, fridges empty, agenda full. Don't lie down now. Look them in the eye. Bring your best thunder. They have set a precedent by overturning laws – the tide may also turn on them with a vengeance, swallowing up their rights and protections.

The door stands ajar for those with the mettle to see where this all started and where it is now. A full loop. Back to women dying on the kitchen floor. Haemorrhaging and vomiting, pale and delirious, life ebbing away. Women whose choice has been wrestled away WILL resort to self-induced abortion. Bloodied needle. Bottle of gin. Punch to the gut. Then sepsis. A risky rendezvous and back street chemicals – profit for the drug dealer who moved into the space where healthcare should have been. If you criminalise abortion, women will still do it. That's two deaths now.

We bear the crushing burden of birthing humanity, the pain, the blood, because that is what we have always done. Women have cried enough tears to fill many seas because no other part of the human body has been politicised or colonised as much as the human womb. We women – in touch with the amniotic power of the ocean, in touch with the amniotic power deep within ourselves – will never be irresponsible enough to put the womb on the front line in the battle for human rights. Until you bleed like we do, you cannot tell us what to do with our bodies.

Tears of blood drop to the page as we write love letters to our wombs. Don't worry, Womb, we will look after you. They may spit their venom onto your petals but we all know toxic masculinity is far more fragile than you will ever be. Perhaps this is why they treat you like a machine, forcing you into pregnancies you cannot bear. We will stand with you when you say "no," because it is your choice and yours alone.

Life expectancy is shorter under patriarchal rule. Without even thinking about the consequences, you thieved women's choice then bred your wives and daughters to exhaustion, until the orphanages were full and the traffickers and abusers circled. That is not pro-life. That is pro-irresponsible. If our Goddess and your God thought men worthy to incubate lives and have control of the birth process, She would have put the womb in men. She didn't. Nor did he. Get over it.

"Shut up and put out," they said.

If patriarchy is right to seize power of women's bodies, why set an impossible standard that completely goes against nature – a silent woman on a pedestal, a host womb AND a virgin? It's all nonsense, isn't it?

The fall of Roe feels like a witch hunt. We've been here before. But this time round we ask this question,

"If you were right to snatch control of the female body, how come you spent 2,000 years murdering women to prove it?"

The other side of war is the war patriarchy wages at home – against its own mothers, wives, daughters, sisters, friends and colleagues. We all know when male energy is out of balance it gets toxic, chaotic and erratic. When male energy is under threat it goes into attack mode. *So why attack women's rights now? Why criminalise vulnerable women facing hard decisions?* Is it because capitalist patriarchy is out of ideas and, when under threat, needs easy victories?

It'll never end, will it? You'll never be able to keep your hooks and chains away from our wombs. But we see you Patriarchy. We see how you want us exhausted and powerless. We see how you wrap your barbed wire around our wombs and pull it tight. We see you for what you are – playground bullies, in escalation mode, hands like nets, swiping at cobwebs and dusty old texts, trying to justify crushing women for the millionth time, which quite frankly is getting wearisome.

Veiled in sea mist, teardrops falling on ink, we write love letters to our embryos, asking if they want to be born into this broken world, because no one asks what the Third Voice wants.

Patriarchy uses the Third Voice to justify attacking the First Voice – the mother. Consider this: Maybe our embryos prefer to leave this world to save their mother, having done their job on Earth this time around. Perhaps our embryos are waiting to be reborn into a less divisive, more holistic and peaceful world, where their mothers are not attacked for being female. Perhaps, like us, they long for a world where birth is not weaponised.

Silver sunlight shimmers as soft as moonlight and vapour hangs above the water. The sea is still. It moves like mercury, mirroring 'Our Own Divine' back to us. Porcelain fingers rippling the surface, we swim back to a time when God was a woman. We swim through the mist towards a cave in a distant sea stack where the sirens, mermaids and sea serpents are waiting. Lilith, the first woman and the first woman to say NO is here. Eve, the second woman and issuer of the first commandment, 'eat the apple' – the bite that shook patriarchy to its core – is here. The midwives; the cord cutters; the arbiters of destiny; the Hydra; the dragons; the primordial sea monsters; the ones who came first; the defenders of our caves – all of them female – all of them demonised by patriarchy – all of them powerful – all are here. So is Hecate.

In this cave far out at sea, we invoke Hecate, ancient medicine Goddess of the underground moon, conduit for the female voice and gatekeeper to the sacred womb. Divinely authorised and protected by Her thundering hounds, Hecate has stood at the crossroads with women making major decisions for millions of years, gifting us choice, our key to freedom. Here we sip the tea, lie down on a bed made with Yew fronds and set sail on waves of sovereignty, from the cave of female mysteries to the sea of nymphs – women's space.

This is Goddess space. This is ancient space. What happens here is not your concern. Keep out. You are not welcome here.

Hecate

Kat Shaw

blood red

Julie A. Dickson

fear
        I am dying
please hurt me no more
stripped, pinned down
I scream – squeezed shut
eyes won't see, smell faces
        too close

shame
        I am crying
curl up, blood red, bruised
lifted – mama's arms cradle
she cries, loudly, cleansed
        but not gone

anger
        no doctor help
I lay stripped again, white sheet
like shroud – pain deep in belly
something's wrong
        I am dying

Hear My Cries

Julie A. Dickson

Whispers surround me as rustling
leaves, vermilion blood dribbles
reaching down like so many rivulets

to earth, join Gaia – she will enfold
me again, ancient knowledge now
forbidden, *return to me daughter*

as my life flows out, Pachamama
hear my cries, men do not know
what they have done mother, I go

Autonomy

Kat Shaw

Regaining Bodily Sovereignty For All: A Birthright

Dr. Denise Renye

I, like many, repeatedly took comfort in the sense of bodily autonomy and freedom that the U.S. Supreme Court case *Roe v. Wade* provided, so when it was overturned, I was shocked, enraged, and dismayed. How and why it happened was clear – a rise in conservatism and the Republican party stacking the court with conservative justices when vacancies arose – but that didn't make it any easier to digest. I also think it happened due to control and fear. Fear that women will indeed be sovereign beings. Fear that women's bodies could not be controlled and/or sexualized and objectified the way they have been in the past. It's fear of the Divine Feminine rising to Her rightful position of equality. Not everyone wants that.

However, the intellectual understanding of something does not automatically lead to an embodied understanding. Information must be processed through all avenues of comprehension before it can fully be understood. In the aftermath of the Supreme Court's decision, I looked around and noticed something inspiring: How when anger is met with constructive action, it can birth something new or protect something already in existence. I notice, with *Roe v. Wade,* people are rising up and saying "no" to this decision. It's not only in supposedly "liberal" places either. For instance, in Kansas, voters decided in the summer of 2022 whether to keep the 2019 state constitutional amendment protecting abortion or not. Nearly 60% of voters wanted to preserve abortion protections and 900,000 voters turned out for the primary election, which accounts for nearly half of all registered voters, the *Guardian* reported. Those numbers usually aren't seen during a primary election, only a general election! People are motivated. They care. They are voicing, "I have a right to sovereignty over my body."

We can and will take our power back to transform our society. In fact, it is necessary to do so! Authority figures need to know their actions are expressly not OK and we're not taking the overturning of *Roe v. Wade* without a strategic, constructive, and intelligent fight. We see this with the situation surrounding Florida Rep. Matt Gaetz. He attempted to humiliate a young woman via Twitter by saying he thinks overweight and unattractive women, a category in which he placed her, don't need to worry about getting pregnant or needing abortions. The target of his attack, 19-year-old political activist Olivia Julianna, used the opportunity to not only put Gaetz in his place but also raise more than $700,000 for abortion care, *NPR* reported. Essentially, the money goes to support the freedom to choose what happens to one's body. Julianna expressed her anger and used it as fuel for a cause she cares about. She actively stood up to a man who needs to be intervened upon because he has allegedly been a predator to underage girls for his own sexual desires. Someone who is a predator automatically uses manipulation as a way to take someone else's choice away. Statutory rape, and all rape, is the opposite of having sovereignty over one's own body.

Julianna and other activists demonstrate we will not passively sit back. We will use our voices. It is with the Divine Feminine energy of the likes of the Hindu Goddess of death and rebirth, Kali, that we can embody our rage in useful and helpful ways. We can embrace the anger within and transform it into political activism, holding space either in peer counseling or as licensed psychologists or psychotherapists, creating or joining women's circles, or even multi-gendered circles if the space is considered sacred and safe for such a conglomeration of people.

The *Roe v. Wade* ruling is not only about abortion; it's very much about sovereignty in general. Did you know that before 1972, single women were denied access to the birth control pill? They had to pretend to be married or engaged in order to receive a prescription and/or submit a note signed by a parent or a clergy member giving her permission, as though she were a child. Reproductive rights are always about control; of women, yes, but also trans men because some of them also have the capacity to carry a child. However, this ruling helps us to have a larger picture in mind and we must deepen our understanding of body sovereignty beyond women. Not only do bodies and psyches of women suffer from such antiquated governmental rulings that do anything but separate church and state, but men and how they suffer from these patriarchal laws is also important.

Male bodies and psyches also suffer and are integral in the recovery of sovereignty for all. Following the first wave of feminism, there was a sort of man-bashing or hatred of men, for understandable reasons. It was necessary to place the blame on a concrete "other." Many women go through a stage in their own development of self that may include making men "bad" or "wrong." How to make sense of these feelings though? It is true the laws have been made by men, however, in the evolution of self it is important to consider how even those who made the laws have been at the mercy of the greater damaging paradigm of patriarchy. Author and activist bell hooks captured this beautifully in her book *The Will to Change: Men, Masculinity, and Love* when she notes, "Within the early writings of radical feminism, anger, rage, and even hatred of men was voiced, yet there was no meaningful attempt to offer ways to resolve these feelings."

To have an acceptance and understanding of all feelings within is important because otherwise you're living in deep discomfort or acting in self-harming ways. It's paramount to have a way to assimilate feelings in the lived experience. There must be room for women to embody their rage and, again, it is understandable that men are the focus of this because of their social conditioning: They are the main character vehicles through which, and from which, the danger of patriarchy emanates. It is a task of mammoth proportion for this all to change. hooks continued to illustrate the sad and scary state of affairs in stating the most painful truth of male domination: "Men wield patriarchal power in daily life in ways that are awesomely life-threatening; that women and children cower in fear and various states of powerlessness, believing that the only way out of their suffering, their only hope is for men to die, for the patriarchal father not to come home."

Many women (and non-traditional men and nonbinary folx) with whom I work in therapy, teaching, and coaching contexts, can relate to this. I know I can too. One cannot be a woman or non-traditional man or anything in between and not have experienced the fear associated with male dominance, at least minimally, in their lifetime. To move from paralyzing fear to embracing anger and the energy of demand is helped by seeing ways in which cis men are making changes. For instance, after the Supreme Court's decision, some men shared memes or discussed their vasectomy stories. And the interest in vasectomy is growing. New data from Innerbody Research found Google searches for "how much is a vasectomy" and "are vasectomies reversible" are up 250% since the Supreme Court leak, according to *Jezebel.com*.

Also, daily searches that include the term "vasectomy" are up 99% from 6,033 average searches per day between March 6 and April 2, to 12,000 from May 1 to May 7, *Jezebel* revealed. The states where searches for "vasectomy near me" were most popular were Michigan, Kentucky, Indiana, Ohio, and Florida. Nearly all of these states have pre-*Roe* abortion bans or "trigger bans" that automatically banned abortion once *Roe* no longer applied, or other stringent abortion bans and restrictions already in effect. When it comes to sexism, the onus for dismantling it falls on people who identify as women. However, that doesn't actually work for the greater good of all. A *Harvard Business Review* article found when people who identify as men are deliberately engaged in gender inclusion programs, 96% of organizations see progress, compared with only 30% of organizations where men are not engaged. The article authors W. Brad Johnson and David G. Smith wrote, "Individualistic approaches to solving gender inequities overlook systemic structural causes and reinforce the perception that these are women's issues. In essence, men are told they don't need to be involved. Without the avid support of men, often the most powerful stakeholders in most large corporations, significant progress toward ending gender disparities is unlikely."

Without the support of men, significant progress toward advancing issues that affect people who identify as women are unlikely, whether that's reproductive choice or punishing sexual crimes. Including men, understanding their importance and how they are also affected by patriarchy, may make it easier to move from hating the actual men themselves to seeing them as living and breathing parts of a larger, dangerous, systemic issue. We are provided a potential solution by hooks: "To love boys rightly we must value their inner lives enough to construct worlds, both private and public, where their right to wholeness can be constantly celebrated and affirmed, where their need to love and be loved can be fulfilled." This is a tall order, especially when we women feel unseen, unheard, and disrespected by the men that used to be the boys who were not loved properly. I don't write this with all the answers to an ancient problem, but I do write this with an offering to honor your internal world, create space for all that is arising, and all your personal evolution to occur within. It is only then that bodily sovereignty will become a reality for all.

References

Chang, Alvin. "Kansas abortion referendum drives record number of voters to polls." *The Guardian*. August 3, 2022.

Cheung, Kylie. "Vasectomy Searches Are Up 250% Since the Roe v. Wade Leak." *Jezebel.com*. May 10, 2022.

hooks, bell. The *Will to Change: Men, Masculinity, and Love* (1st ed.) New York: Washington Square Press, 2004.

Johnson, W. Brad; Smith, David G. "How Men Can Become Better Allies to Women." *Harvard Business Review*. October 12, 2018.

Jones, Dustin. "A Texas teen raises over $700,000 for abortions after Rep. Matt Gaetz mocked her." *NPR*. July 28, 2022.

Song: Sovereign

Molly Remer

No one shall take my power,
no one shall govern me,
I am wild in my wisdom,
I am strong
and I am free.
Sovereign of body,
sovereign of soul,
I am sacred,
I am whole.

Goddess of the Heart

Arna Baartz

Ungovernable

Molly Remer

We will not settle into subjugation.
We are here,
claiming our power
and celebrating our magic,
and refusing to surrender our joy.
We are whole
and we are here.
We are free,
our sovereignty inviolate,
ungovernable.

Denied

Kat Shaw

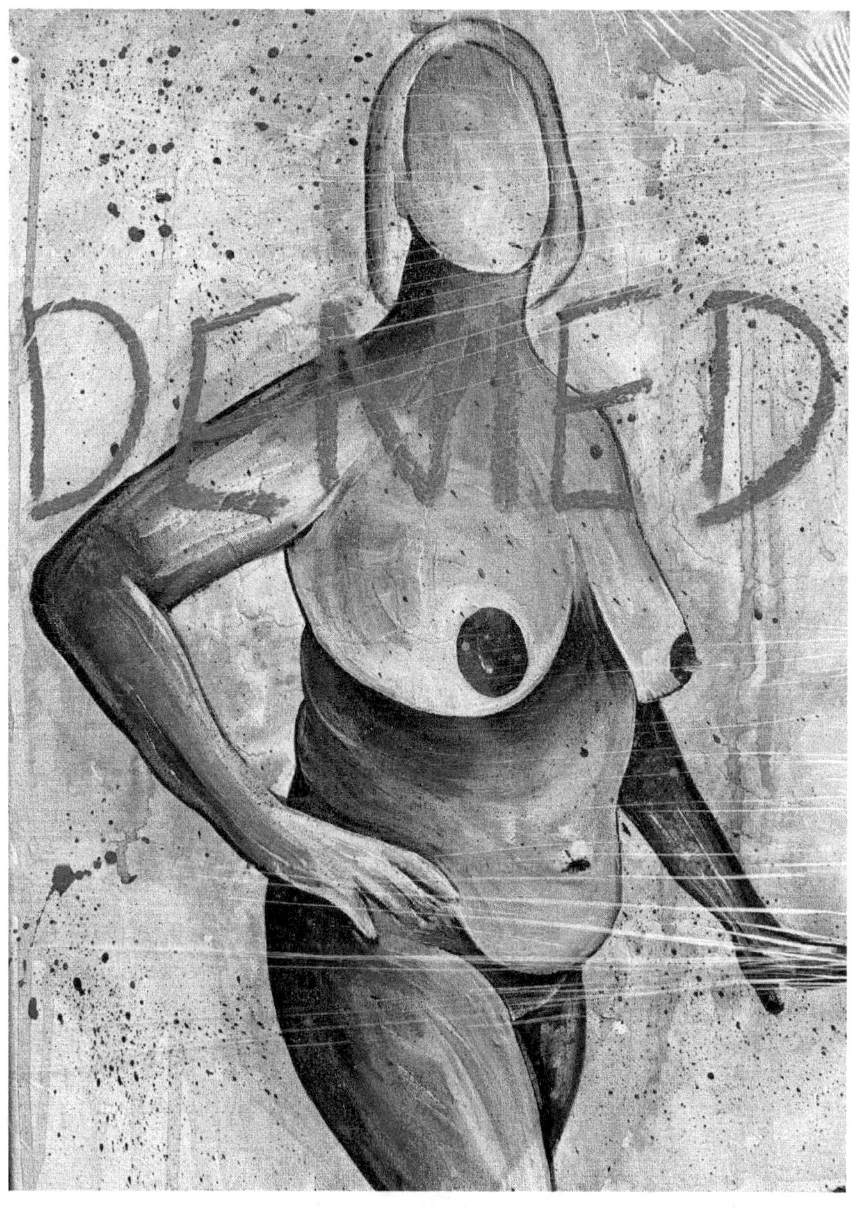

BOTH LIFE AND CHOICE

Jodi Blazek Gehr

March for Life, 1978

Earlier than I would get up for school and before the snowy roads were cleared, an eager catechism teacher drove a friend and me through a snowstorm to walk in the March for Life, an annual event opposing both the practice and legality of abortion, culminating with a rally at our State Capitol. In my sixth-grade CCD class (circa 1978), I had recently learned about abortion and was taught that, unequivocally, it was wrong.

I learned that morning that not everyone sees abortion, or pro-life issues, the same way. I was stunned as we entered the Capitol that there were women already positioned on the balconies, holding signs, and shouting at marchers about having rights to their own bodies. It left me very confused—a woman's body is different than an unborn baby, I thought, and yet there was such passion, so much anger.

As an outspoken pro-life teenager, I was so sure of what I understood about abortion that in 1984 I wrote a letter to the editor of the *Daily Nebraskan*, my college newspaper. I pulled that old newspaper out of storage a few days after Roe vs. Wade was overturned. Nearly four decades later, I am uneasy with what I wrote. What I used to be so sure of, I am now less certain of and often, in complete disagreement with my younger self.

What I have learned since then about life and choice.

Two things can be true at the same time. I believe BOTH that human life is sacred from the time of conception AND that we are created to have free will. We have agency over our own bodies, choosing whether our life continues and/or whether we will bring life forth. Embracing a culture of life is respecting not just the unborn child, but also the pregnant woman while advocating for issues including prenatal care, childcare, gender equality, trafficking, healthcare reform, gun safety, racism, climate change, LGBTQ rights, capital punishment, and so much more.

Identifying as pro-choice or pro-life is a false dichotomy that limits the possibility of discussion. Advocating for the legal right to choose may not mean that one is pro-abortion, but that one believes that women should be trusted to make that decision, not the government. Despite political efforts to force us to choose sides, there is a third way, a both/and perspective, that includes more expansive, nuanced, and compassionate attitudes, behavior, and policies.

We live in a pluralistic society with many religious beliefs; not everyone agrees about the morality or legality of abortion. According to the First Amendment, it is unconstitutional to impose one's religious beliefs on others; the United States was founded on the separation of church and state. Despite the belief by many that life begins at conception, it is not held by all religions. Some believe life begins at quickening or the first breath.

> "The *Torah*, the *Mishnah*, the *Talmud* and later rabbinic sources consider the woman's physical and emotional health before that of the fetus. Until the baby is born, Judaism considers the fetus to be part of the woman's body. She is never the villain when difficult choices need to be made." –Rabbi Mara Nathan

I cannot imagine the difficult circumstances that would warrant a pregnancy termination or what a forced pregnancy or birth would feel like. Forcing compliance with laws prohibiting abortion is a clear violation of human rights and could very well compromise a woman's mental, physical, and spiritual health. A "crime against humanity," according to the United Nations includes rape, sexual slavery, enforced prostitution, forced pregnancy, enforced sterilization or any other form of sexual violence of comparable gravity. Just as one cannot be forced to love another, a woman cannot be forced to embrace the sacred mystery of pregnancy, childbirth, and parenting without her whole mind, body, and spirit being on board. Legal mechanisms, power, and oppression—efforts to push an agenda or a belief on another—never result in peace.

Sacred Fire

Danielle Boodoo-Fortune

This is My Body

Molly Remer

I love life.
I love women.
I love babies.
I love people
and want them
to flourish and thrive.
I believe pregnancy is magic,
birth is beautiful,
and wombs are miracle-makers.
I believe children are a gift
and life is holy.
AND,
this is my body,
inviolate.
This body belongs to me,
self-sovereign and whole.
I claim my right
to choose my way,
to inhabit myself fully
and completely
without fear or coercion.
This is my body, my temple.
I am my own sacred space
and I shall not be colonized
by another's will.
It is possible to hold both/and,
to BE both/and,
to hold holy yes
and sacred no as
precious and inalienable
rights of our own free hearts,
bodies, wills, and souls.
Blessed be my body,

sacred site of life and passion.
Blessed be my body,
sacred site at which I say,
"no more."

Her Body, Her Choice

Sionainn McLean

There's a rising tide of rage in me. For so long, we – those with a uterus (and whether that uterus worked or not!) – have been told in both subtle and not so subtle ways that we are only worth the contents of said uterus. Those that choose not to have kids are just "confused". Those that fill it with life, are sacred objects to be protected, though incapable of making decisions, until it's expelled – and then we return to our state of prude or slut, depending on our proclivities to obey and not question. Even married, in a monogamous relationship, a woman who gets an abortion is called a whore. Even if it was to save her life, she's a murderer and selfish. Not that abortion should ever be limited to that extreme of "oh, she could die, I guess it's ok this time." Our body, our choice.

When we give birth, society lets us know that it doesn't matter if it was traumatic, it only matters that the baby survived. Whether women walk out, or are wheeled out in a wheelchair, or in a coffin, it doesn't matter – that's just "how it is." If we leave behind our once healthy bodies, our other children, our lovers and partners, our parents and siblings, our friends, our dreams, goals, and life itself, it's just a tragic reality. It's a woman's place, to die in blood and pain, to exchange her life for another's. As long as we did our "duty" of producing another little human, the world can rejoice in "life," – even if the coin is a woman's suffering and death.

Because we know in our society that our children will always be cared for – given shelter, food, clothing, not knowing misery and suffering, given an education, and lifted on high. No child in America knows homelessness, starvation, or abuse. No child is told they are lesser because of the circumstance of their birth, the color of their skin, or their reproductive bits. Not like those "uncivilized" countries.

Do I need to point out my sarcasm? Because I feel like I do. I feel like I'm screaming at a wall. I feel like those of us who know, that understand and see, that walk with a Goddess who is balanced with a

God, and not just a God who has never been balanced with a Goddess are screaming at walls and rocks. The walls that want to lock women into rooms on their knees, and the rocks that can only reiterate what's been told to them, the lies and the emotional response… "Oh won't someone please think of the children?"

We are more than our bodies, and yet we have fewer rights than a corpse. No one can take healthy body parts from a corpse – no matter how much someone needs a kidney or a heart or a lung – you need permission from the dead or their family. Why is it right that a woman be forced to carry something that will affect her body and her life for 9 months? Why must she risk her life because someone else has determined that the clump of cells that took two people to make (and only one of which gets punished) is more important than her? She's there, living, breathing. It's her body.

HER BODY.

I have a uterus, and I have children. I chose that path. I was lucky never to have had to make that choice. I know it's not an easy one, but it is a necessary one that all with a uterus should have. I have two daughters and I will fight with every ounce of myself to protect their rights to make that choice. It's their bodies. It's their choice. No one, and I mean NO ONE will ever make that choice for them, or take that choice away. This is the hill I would die on. I cannot fathom the fact that there's a risk that my daughters might have fewer rights than I did. That they must fight for these rights like their grandmothers, and grandmother's mothers. How is this right? How can we let ourselves go backwards?

We know it's not about babies and children. It's about control. It's about a religion believing their way of life, their perspective, **is** the only right way. And forcing that view on others, even though their holy book says nothing on this issue. In fact, their god has been the cause of infanticide several times. So much for right to life.

We have entered another dark age – a 10-year-old girl, raped by her own father, forced to carry and give birth. We know what that will do to her body, her already traumatized mind and her spirit. They don't care. A mother, with already breathing children, forced to carry and give birth, although she's been told giving birth again will kill her — even if she used birth control. It doesn't matter that no birth control is 100% — a woman who has sex must be punished! While a man can have as much sex as he likes (and father as many children as he wants without taking care of them), even a responsible woman who loves her husband isn't allowed to enjoy sex. Because for her, sex is only for procreation, right? The poor couple that wanted a child desperately — more than anything else in the world — is forced to suffer as the woman carries a dead fetus that could kill her. Late term miscarriages are aided with medical procedures that are considered abortion procedures, even though the trauma that occurs and the risk to her life is serious. Anyone claiming that a woman uses late term abortions as birth control, or just decides that she made this decision on a whim is a deluded liar. No one, and I mean NO ONE does that. Late term abortion is a devastating medical decision every time.

It's all asinine. It's hateful, controlling and it's all a lie. It can't be allowed in a society that claims *freedom*. It's oppression, it's slavery — women are not chattel. We've long endeavored and worked for equality, and the Supreme Court's decision to overturn Roe v Wade is a slap in the face to our ancestor mothers who fought. It's a turning of the clocks, to send women back in time.

Most important, it's wrong. Our Goddesses are raging with us. Those who work to take away our sovereignty will not find us to be meek and demure handmaidens. We are the children of all Goddesses, including war Goddesses The Morrigan, Kali, Artemis, Freyja, Astarte, Athena, Sekhmet, Innanna — to name a few — all lifting us to claim our crowns, our sovereignty — the right to make choices for our own bodies — whether that's to have or not have children, to have abortions, to have sex, to dress in the way that makes us most happy, to live, to dream, to prosper. It's all related, it's all part of the same package labeled *freedom*.

And while we want to weep (we can!) and rage (we should!) — we have to fight, we have to take all this painful energy and direct it — by voting. This is how we stand up in a democracy. Because if that doesn't work, nothing short of war will.

Fury

Kat Shaw

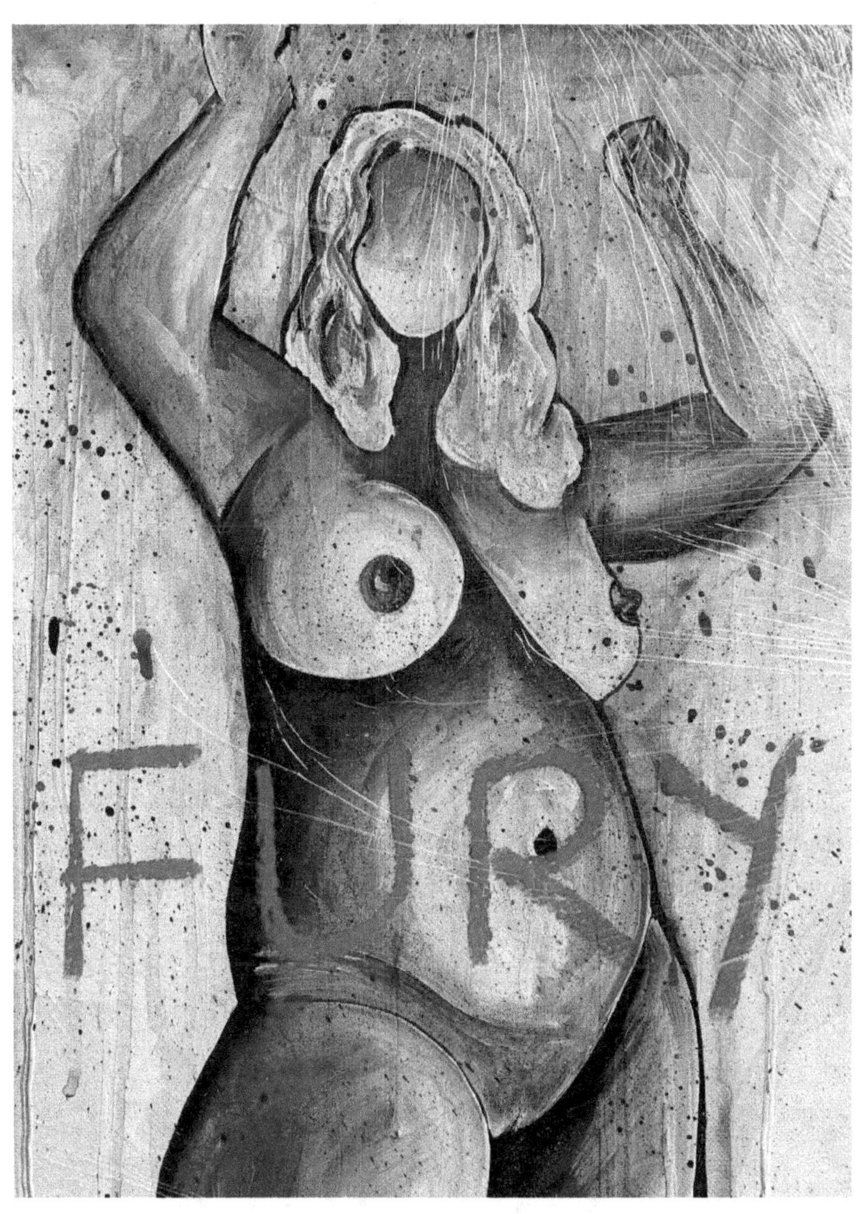

We're Not Your Chattel, We're Not Your Cattle!

Sharon Smith

I've just heard,
You're trying to make us a HERD;
Strip away our bodily autonomy
Bring us under your strict authority.

But we're NOT your Chattel,
And we're NOT your Cattle.

How dare you treat us like we are!
Like we exist to be bought, branded, and BRED
by You and your Misogynistic Minions,
With no say in the matter.

You laugh as our bellies get fatter and fatter,
And you "Cock-your-Doodle-Do" and
strut around, as if birthing is all about YOU.
Well, it isn't!

Never has been; never WILL be.
"Our Bodies, Our Choice,"
we boldly proclaim as you take aim
At our Sovereignty, our right to self-determination
In Human Germination.

Yet you seek to punish us
When we choose to abort;
It's often our last resort
In order to stay alive, to live and thrive;

But you wage your unholy battle
Because you want us to be your Cattle!

Breeding stock...
Milkers...
Poke us and inseminate us,
Make us carry your "seed"

You just want us to breed!

But we're NOT your Chattel;
And we're NOT your Cattle.

And we're fighting back:
You've unleashed a Whirlwind,
Opened Pandora's Box,
Awakened Medusa,
Pissed off Artemis.

And now we're coming for you, GOP...
"Grand Ol' Patriarchs, Grabbin' Our Pussies."
We're coming after you:
A stampede to be freed
from your tyranny...and your greed.

You don't own us.

We're NOT your Chattel;
And we're NOT your Cattle.

We're coming for you, Far Right Christianity,
With your religious Insanity
Forcing upon us your beliefs,
Causing unnecessary pain and grief.

Wanting us to submit to men,
To always be "lesser-than"
Your misogyny is showing...

And our rage is growing.

Keep your fucking hands off our Wombs!
We alone have the right to decide
Whether they'll be incubators, or tombs.

YOU don't get a say!

Because
WE are NOT your Chattel,
And WE are NOT your Cattle.

We refuse to be
Objects of your misogyny
Condemned by your
Religious insanity

We choose our AUTONOMY.

We stand in our Sovereignty!

We will be FREE!

My Body, My Choice

Kat Shaw

Ride the Rage Wave

Gina Martin

Rage. Holy sacred rage. Fire-tossed and torrent-flooded rage. Enough rage awakened from thousands of years of oppression to match and overcome the fury of misogynistic patriarchy.

I'm three years old and my father shoves my mother across the bed I am lying in and holds her against the wall by the throat. I think I am screaming, but maybe not. Maybe I am too terrified to make a sound.

I am five years old, and I am with my mother walking the neighborhood, canvassing for the League of Women Voters. If a man answered the door, I remember the wall of fury that would hit us when mom asked if the woman of the house was registered to vote. Slammed doors would be the response.

I am eight years old, and my mother goes to Father McNulty, the young, cool, hip priest, asking for his help and support. She has a black eye. He tells her it is her responsibility to make her marriage work.

I am nine years old, and my father asks my mother who she voted for (Goldwater vs. Johnson). She replies 'Johnson' and my father breaks her nose. That was the day I became a Democrat.

Then we add on the impossible weight of Eve's guilt and the omnipresent burden of original sin. Being a woman is a constant state of hiding from male judgment and anger. Violence against women is ignored and accepted. Ah, the 50's and 60's in America.

But gradually, things began to shift. The Pill. The Feminist movement. Women breaking the glass ceilings in higher education and professional careers.

I am eighteen years old and have had unprotected sex with my first lover. My mother, for a litany of reasons too long to count, had a "never I hate it" attitude about sex. So, I, in my 'hey, it's the sexual liberation' back-sided philosophy, had adopted a weird sense of righteousness about how I would never say "no". Like some bizarre badge of honor. That was a tense fraught two weeks waiting for my period. The sheer terror of what might be happening. The absolute blank mind about what I could do if 'it' did happen. And then, the quick trip to Planned Parenthood for the Pill.

The tipping point of 1973-74. Women getting their own bank accounts and credit cards. My mother saying, "Women who marry rich men earn every penny." For me, for all of us, financial autonomy meant choice. Freedom to move, leave, dream, choose. It was heady. Choice. And then came body autonomy with

Roe.

Roe.

ROE.

It didn't get easy, it just got easier. But the sovereign right to our own bodies went a long way to letting us believe that the inequities of the past were soon going to be history. We were wrong. We misjudged the tenacious grip of the existing power structures. We let ourselves breathe more deeply. We let our shoulders fall down from around our ears. We looked forward and forgot to watch our backs.

Younger women believed the battle for gender equality was won. They looked forward to new battles, new horizons. Gender fluidity, transgender rights, non-binary self-definitions, all noble causes, became the forefront of concern for the millennials and the Gen Z's. I didn't want my daughter to ever know that paralyzing terror of an unwanted and uncontrolled possible pregnancy. Why should she and her peers hold the fear inside them that we had known. It was better for them. Better that they *not* know how bad it had been. Part of me was frustrated when they didn't acknowledge how tortuously difficult it had been for centuries. The ease of their liberty and the nonchalance that came with it stung sometimes. But still, it was better, yes?

Some of us old crones were still hollering, "Don't forget about the women!" Or to quote Jane Adams, "Don't forget about the ladies." Or to quote Hildegard of Bingen or Hypatia or Jean d'Arc.

But…. we forgot to do what women have done for 5,000 years– We forgot to
Watch. Our. Backs.
For again, as has been true since the onslaught of patriarchy, it is the women who suffer the most.

So- rage.

Yes, holy mother of god, holy mother, great mother, mother of us all- RAGE.

I tremble when I try to speak about how the loss of body sovereignty is affecting me, how it will affect my daughter, all our daughters.

I feel the need to find the primordial wave of rage deep, deep within myself. I know that wave connects us all. If we, one by one, tap into that wave, call out to our sisters and brothers, attempt to stand up on that wave and ride it. What a ride that will be!

Holy Mother of us all, teach me how to harness that sacred rage. Show me the power and righteousness of creative fury. Guide me to be

She who Holds the Spear of Justice

She who Protects the Women

She who Never Yields

She Who Stands against the Tide of Repression

She who Stands

She Who Stands

SHE WHO STANDS

Andraste

Kat Shaw

The Soul of Woman

Arlene Bailey

For days I've been sick – literally – from the collective energy surrounding the current attack on women. Sure, I could call it the current political climate, but in truth it is the ultimate assault on women and women's rights.

We. Do. Not. Matter.

Not just in the grand scheme of things, but – to these men – we do not matter at all. We are merely an impediment meant to be stomped on, an irritant to shackle and control, if not completely eradicate.

AND...

Women ARE Rising. I know this. I see this. Sadly, though, as long as these privileged white men have the power they have and the monetary support that holds them in place, our battle is far from over. In fact, it is becoming larger and larger. As women, we HAVE come a long way in changing things, but if we think our fight is over or less, then we are not paying attention. It's about to get a whole lot worse.

AND...

As I've read in many places from other writers, Patriarchy has just awakened the Sleeping Dragon... Kali... Lilith... the Morrigan... Sekhmet... Pele... the Amazon. By their callous disregard of women and women's lives and safety, they have called forth Boudicca, the Iceni Queen who raged against the Romans for killing her husband and raping her daughters. Just. Because. They. Could. *Sound familiar?*

However, now each of us is reaching our tipping point.

For me, it was a few days ago and, as often happens with a tipping point, it began with an irritating, but insignificant (in the grand scheme of things) event. Through it all, what, or rather who, kept coming to mind was Boudicca. I kept thinking what she'd do. Not just about this stupid event that was my tipping point, but about all the insidiousness happening to women at the moment. The only words that made any sense in my cluttered mind – the only ones clear – were "Boudicca Rises." Then more words began to come and I knew that phrase was bigger than a mere passing thought.

Like a wraith raised from a haunted rest, Boudicca would not go away... her sword cutting through all the thoughts, all the feelings, all the bullshit until she had my tears, my rage, my full-bodied attention. Every hair on my arms, my head, raised like antennas sensing, feeling. Words pulsing through my brain like an emotional hurricane until I knew what was coming. Knew what was birthing. She. SHE. Boudicca. The raging Queen of the Iceni was rising through me and she would have her say... have her wrath expressed... on the page... on the canvas.

But first the tears and words had to flow outward into the void...

"I write with a broken heart, though I do not know why. I have good things in my life, good people. Some of both really good. Then why do I feel this rage building and my heart cracking wide open? Why do I feel lower than the lowest worm? Why do I *not* matter? Why am I scorned and spit at and revolting to so many?"

It is because I,
a woman,
exist.

Not that I exist
here or there,
but that I simply exist.

Why did I choose to come to this time, this fu*@king time, as a woman? Have I not been ridiculed enough in previous lifetimes? Have I not been murdered and tortured, burned and buried alive before? Why risk that again?

There is a primal scream in me this time. A primal rising that says NO MORE!

All I hear in my soul is BOUDICCA RISES!

And so SHE comes. Sword in hand with a death scream that rends the very fabric of the cosmos. Patriarchy came for my daughters once... had its way with them and then tossed them aside... killed my beloved and took my crown. Well, not this time. Not as long as my hands hold a sword and my voice speaks. Not as long as women continue to wake up – really pay attention – and use their voices.

Make no mistake, we are at war – not just for the soul of women, but for the soul of Lady Liberty and America and, indeed for every woman on this planet, including Mother Earth herself. We are at war and it is going to take commitment from every woman, every girl, every man who stands with us.

Each individual who will commit to the idea of NOT ON MY WATCH...

Each woman who will stand and shout...

I AM WOMAN.
I WILL BE SEEN.
I WILL BE HEARD.

Each woman who listens as
Boudicca rises within
and The Morrigan screeches.
As Kali wails and
Pele spews forth her fire.

Each woman who listens as
her own tears fall
raising the wraith within.

Each woman who allows
the primal scream,
adding her own experience,
her own unique voice.

Each woman who listens.
Each woman who sees.
Each woman willing to act.

Listen Sister.
Listen.

For the soul of woman
is on the auction block.

Changing Current

Danielle Boodoo-Fortune

Let Them Hear Us

Nina Gyorgy

Roe v. Wade was overturned two months after I was raped in college. As the news of the repeal washed over me in June of 2022, I was left sobbing in a coworker's lap. I was sent into a playback loop of fractured memories of my assault, hospitalization, and pregnancy tests. Part of me hoped that if I let my eyes blur out my reality for a moment, just maybe I would wake up in a different one.

I hope to never again see the shock and emotional strain that I witnessed in this group of summer camp counselors after our boss informed us of the Supreme Court's decision. Watching as arms began to wrap around one another, faces began to melt, smiles disappeared, and tears rolled down every cheek, I knew we were experiencing generational trauma.

Our camp community sat in this feeling for a little under an hour. The silence was broken by jokes of how we could try to poison members of the court, but no amount of dark humor could relieve this kind of ache.

Beneath the sadness I found a moment of clarity: we could all grieve here together, find comfort in our similar reactions, but none of us will ever understand the extent or root of another's pain. Here lies the importance of sharing our stories.

● ● ●

The day after I was raped, I walked into the campus police department holding a paper bag containing my vomit-stained clothes and blood-stained sheets from the day before. I had been told to shut up and keep my head down more than enough times in my life to know that this time I was going to be heard.

Boston College has 3 times the amount of reported cases of rape than its competing schools, but the widely accepted truth was that no one wins their assault case here, that this isn't a school known for believing women.

The date of my trial was set for August. I had chosen to pursue a Title IX violation against my rapist. I knew that with what I had to say, even if I didn't win the case, there was no way they wouldn't believe me. Here lies my opening statement:

• • •

Have you ever tried to take a picture of the moon? Even when it's full in the sky, trying to capture it with a mere image makes it look small, insignificant. It's the same with every rape case. You can look at all of the evidence, hear my voice shake and quiver as you press me on the details, but you will never fully understand what it was like for me to be there, in that moment.

You can ask a million questions, but nothing changes the fact that I was incapacitated and he was sober. You can refuse to believe that I said no, you can let yourself think that I didn't tell him "I don't want to do this anymore," but he remembers and I remember. Only I know the way he invaded my body and touched my skin without my consent. Only I can know the extent of the pain he caused me.

Have you ever gone swimming in a crystal clear lake? Jumping into the surface of the undisturbed water — everything is peaceful, perfect. Floating in the comfortable abyss, even if something touches your foot, you brush it off, moments ago it was clear as far as the eye could see. Your ears fill with water, your fingers and toes start to prune, but you don't care, you're floating! This is how it feels to have a blood alcohol level over 0.2. Nothing is, nothing was, nothing is going to be, it's only you and this clear water.

Now imagine how it would feel to wake up at the bottom of the lake. You remember every second of sinking, so why didn't you swim? Because when you're the one in the crystal–clear lake, you can't tell water from air. You have no idea that the fish pulling you deeper is slowly killing you .

The funny thing is, I work as a lifeguard – (bet you didn't know that). I've saved a lot of women from the fish lurking in the crystal-clear lake.

I've intervened at parties as I see a woman start to struggle. And I've dealt with the aftermath of pulling someone out after they've hit the bottom. When you're at the bottom with someone looking up – the water is cloudy, you can't see the top, but you start to pull them out anyway. You support their dead weight and hope and pray that they'll wake up and start swimming on their own.

Nobody's the same after getting raped. You lose a sparkle in your eye. Everything is different. You no longer feel safe in your body or your home. It seems like an eternal process, rebuilding the part of me that he broke. Trying to clear the panic attacks and the fear, and the event itself from my brain and body. But I'm here for the long run. And that's why I'm doing this. I have no control over the outcome or how the karma from this event is distributed. All I can do is show up and try to explain to you how it feels to be drowning.

You'll never hear the sobbing phone calls. You'll never see the bloody cotton swabs the nurse took from my vaginal canal. You'll never know the days I struggled to get out of bed, to eat, telling myself to put down the knife, that he'd already caused me enough pain, You won't watch me recover or witness my growth. I only hope that in hearing my story of drowning, Boston College will choose to protect students like me to make campus a place where everyone feels safe. Choose to be on the side that helps me to swim.

● ● ●

Surprisingly enough, in the middle of September I was sent an email that my assaulter was pronounced guilty. His punishment? A semester without classes, then back to business as usual. My own willingness to release this to a higher power allowed me to see that the real justice for this situation came from him having to not only listen to my opening statement and questioning, but to the 17 witnesses that testified to my incapacitated state that day and to his previous objectifications of my body.

By the time I received the news of his conviction, I had already fled over 3,000 miles to Norway for the year, to try to find value in my pain and transmute my suffering into love.

I tell you all of this for pure exposure to one young woman's story of assault. We are taught as little girls in America that our bodies are not our own. Taught that we must behave for boys, dress better, look better, and talk quieter to not disturb the men in our lives. The overturning of Roe v. Wade only highlights this and ingrains it in every female-identifying person in the U.S. The reality of forced births in this country makes every experiencing woman a victim, no matter their conception story. The choice of the Supreme Court to remove women's basic human rights is disgusting, but we the people are stronger than ever. We the people no longer sit quietly. I am able to rest only because I know that they will hear us, they will see us, and change will come because we refuse to be silenced.

Fight
Kat Shaw

Today, I Bleed

C. Ara Campbell

Today, I bleed. For the hundredth day in a row. I am a womb holder with a uterus that is at war with me. I bleed for months at a time, in misery and anguish. And I beg. For relief. For compassion. Please, take this pain from me. Take this organ from me, that betrays my body and fills me with despair.

When I was in my late 20's, I told my previous doctor that I wanted a hysterectomy. To be rid once and for all of the excessive bleeding and the pain that no other solution was able to resolve. It's my body and I don't want children, so it all seemed very logical. Surely, my doctor would hear me. After all, this was my health.

"One day you will want children," my doctor confidently tells me, neglecting my pain completely and focusing only on her opinions for my future. I'm confused as to why she thinks she has authority over my life to make that assumption.

"I won't change my mind. I've never wanted children; my decision was made up a long time ago." I retort, losing patience as I try to barter for the agency of my own body.

"You're young. You will change your mind. Trust me." The doctor repeated, telling me again what I will want.

Angry and frustrated, I continue to plead my case, grasping at any straw I could to get her to take me seriously. "I could always adopt. There are so many children that need a good home. I would love them the same as if I gave birth to them myself." The doctor chuckled, invalidating me once more. That was the end of that conversation, the final decision made for me by someone brainwashed by conservative ideology.

So, I continued to bleed, my body and soul enraged because my agency was not my own. My comfort and health sacrificed upon the altar of the old patriarchal way of thinking. That I, a wishy-washy female, was unable to make such a big decision as this for myself without changing her mind later. Because, according to society, I would want to be a mother eventually. Tormented and in agony, I lay in wait, an incubator forced to endure pain in preparation for something I had never wanted.

The powers that be make laws and regulations to govern bodies that are not their own, considering themselves the rulers of the land we call Self. They deem themselves judge, jury and executioner to control what procedures and medicine we have access to. They choose who will live and who will die. No matter the circumstance of conception, they beat it into us that pregnancy is a blessing. Like cattle, we are bred, forced to keep malfunctioning body parts in case our overlords need to increase the size of their herd. They force us to live with malfunctioning organs or to carry unviable pregnancies to term; thus, they condemn our bodies to be test tubes and graveyards in equal measure.

They call all life precious but don't include us, the unwilling mothers. Who is allowed to make these decisions if not us? The government? Our partners? Do I need a permission slip from a man to confirm I don't want to have children? I am not in elementary school, and this is not a class field trip; this is my fucking body. No one has the right to choose what happens to it but me. Period.

The solution may seem simple to some; find a different doctor that will help you obtain what you require. But, for so many of us, there are little options where we live. Either we dwell in places too rural and unpopulated that there are no services to support us, or doctors align with or are forced to uphold archaic conservative laws and withhold treatment. This is the plight of so many around the globe, limited access to appropriate care. I am one of the lucky ones who was able to find a new doctor who hears and supports me. I refused to see the old doctor again because a healthcare provider that does not understand and uphold freedom of choice is not providing care to the patient. They are propping up a system that considers us chattel and wishes to use us as broodmares.

We are not your fields to sow, to plow and plunder at will. We have the right to choose: what we do with our bodies, how we dress, where we go, how we embody this existence. We have the right to live without fear of forced birth, murder, and abuse.

So, today I bleed, for the rights of us all. Because the powers that be intend for us to bleed for them. To exist in torment and die to birth the next generation of disposable women for them to use. But we will not. I will not permit them to plant their flag upon me. No trespassing is allowed on the sacred ground of my body. They assume we will take things lying down, legs spread, our wills leashed, and our voices gagged. No. We are not your incubators. Their days of control over our bodies and futures need to end.

You'll change your mind, I was told. No. You changed it for me. Like you have done, and plan to do, for all of us. If I was a man, I would have been allowed to choose. Men younger than I was at the time have the autonomy to make that decision for themselves, their agency honored no matter their age or relationship status. What a load of shit. They have the right to choose for their bodies. I demand no less.

Rise up. Let your voice be heard. Support those in power who support us and not the ones who would send us to slaughter. It's not just our reproductive rights they will take away. We're the Uterus in the coal mine; after us, they'll come for you next. They will systematically peel away the rights of anyone they deem a threat to their outdated patriarchal belief system. What was once allowed will be taken away and outlawed. The once free shall be led away in shackles.

They condemn us for what we wear or don't, how we act or where we go, what we do in bed or on the streets. It doesn't matter what we do, we are blamed for their inability to control their actions, their thoughts, their emotions, and their hormones. We are engrained to fear death by their hands and subjugation by their regulations. We are the scapegoats for their toxic masculinity, the punching bag for eons of venomous poison that tries to masquerade itself as manhood.

Their solution is for us to get on our knees and obey. Conform to the rules crafted for their benefit and sold to us covered in our own blood. To shrink ourselves down to a speck of dust to not disrupt their fragile hold on the patriarchal fantasy they cling to. Hide or die. Retreat. Dissolve. Compromise and compact ourselves until we disappear entirely. Fuck that. No more.

So, we fight. For our right to choose. For our autonomy. For our very lives. Our battle cry rises to expel their outdated regulations from our bodies and to cut the chains they have placed upon our freedom once and for all. We are not yours to command. We will not back down or change our minds. Ever.

If I am to bleed, let it be for this.

Abortion Spell

Annie Finch

Let's keep the world through its own balanced kiss,
The kiss come from women made of our own blood,
The holder, the cooler (redeeming the earth,
Shaping the room where we give you your birth).
Hands born of women
Will not stop this flood,
This generous, selfish, long-opening gift.

Salt of Abortion

Annie Finch

After I talked with those thirteen good women
On love and abortion, I noticed the moon's
Golden warm growing. Its crescenting ship
Swung through my ocean, till I rocked in the one
Salt, the one wisdom, we'd woven: our nest.
Held in our silence, I heard us together.
"Abortion is beautiful," crested our voices:
Millions—dead, living, alone, loud together;
Faithful; surviving; strong, supple; true, honest;
Listened to, heard, in the salt courage one
Loving time tended. This presenting ship
Rode through millennia, under tides' moons:
Salt nest, salt courage, salt, weaving, salt, women.

Moon for Our Daughters

Annie Finch

Moon that is linking our daughters'
Choices, and still more beginnings,
Threaded alive with our shadows,

These are our bodies' own voices,
Powers of each of our bodies,
Threading, unbroken, begetting

Flowers from each of our bodies.
These are our spiraling borders
Carrying on your beginnings,

Chaining through shadows to daughters,
Moving beyond our beginnings,
Moon of our daughters, and mothers.

We Have to Have Hope

Raine Shakti

The blood oozed out of the thick pad between my legs as I slowly and painfully walked the mile from the women's health clinic to Kadena Air Base, Japan. Green pay phones dotted my route, but as I'd only been on the island of Okinawa for a month, I hadn't yet figured out how to use them. Walking through the gates of the giant air base, I sank gratefully into the first available cab and gave the address of my apartment. Once home, I staggered through to the bedroom and collapsed gratefully onto my bed. My husband ministered to me for the next two days and took care of our four-month-old while I slept.

I'd found out I was pregnant a month after we'd arrived on base in February 1990. Despite having an infant, I'd said yes to uprooting my family and moving to Kadena to serve as an auditor with the US Air Force. This pregnancy was a surprise. Despite missing a period, I hadn't even considered pregnancy a possibility as my hormones were still erratic after giving birth to my son a few months earlier. A move half-way around the world had added to the burden on my still recovering body so the thought that my husband and I had conceived again had not even crossed my mind.

The nurse practitioner who delivered the news advised me that, due to the Hyde Act, I could not have an abortion on-base, but that abortion was legal in Japan. She provided the number for the clinic, I made an appointment, and my husband took me to the off-base clinic on a Saturday morning. The entrance was on a quiet side street. Despite my nerves, the first thing I noticed was the quiet. There were no protestors calling me a baby killer or blocking my entrance. The procedure itself was only mildly painful and when I awoke from the anesthetic, I was released with heavy pads between my legs and admonished to rest.

Even though the long walk home was painful, I felt a sense of relief that I had been able to exercise my free will.

Although I know I made the right decision for myself and my family, I experienced sorrow over the loss of what could have been my second child. And just as I was supported by the Japanese health care system in having an abortion, I was also supported in the mourning process. The Japanese have a ritual called Mizuko Kuyo, which is a ritual for miscarried or aborted fetuses. The ritual is both an acknowledgement of sorrow and a ritual of faith that the child will be reborn. Although I did not speak Japanese and had no idea where to find a Buddhist temple offering the ritual, a little digging at the on-base library produced an English language version of the ritual. Performing the ritual let me say goodbye, but, more importantly, eased my guilt and helped me to find peace.

Over the years I have reflected periodically on why I felt so much guilt and why abortion was more accepted in Japan than in the United States. What I realized is that, even though I deeply believed I had the right to make the choice which was best for me, and that abortion is not murder, my childhood beliefs had been influenced by the Right-Wing movement's proclamation that women who choose abortion are "baby killers." What I did not realize at the time, but later learned, is that conservatives do not want women to have bodily autonomy because it upends "normal" family structure in which men work and women tend the home. Unfortunately, we have not advanced very far in the 32 years since I had my abortion: In the majority opinion that struck down Roe, Supreme Court Justice Samuel Alito constrained women once again to their reproductive capabilities when he lamented the reduction in the "domestic supply of infants" since abortion became legal.

The second question, why abortion is more accepted in Japan than in the United States, comes down to moral and religious beliefs. Many Americans, especially Right-Wing conservatives, believe that every fetus should be carried to term, regardless of the circumstances surrounding its birth or its prospects for a healthy life. Currently the news is full of stories of women who were denied abortions even when the fetuses were not viable, and those who were forced to prolong their pregnancies until their own health was compromised. The Japanese, who are influenced by Buddhist beliefs, have a more nuanced view of life and death and believe that although an abortion is a "necessary suffering," it is worse to endanger the life of the mother than to bring an unwanted child into the world.

The Mizuko Kuyo ceremony was the beginning of my healing process, but understanding that not every country or culture believes abortion is wrong or that every woman who has an abortion deserves to burn in hell was liberating. I knew when I had my abortion that before Roe desperate women had died from back-alley abortions and the use of coat hangers to perform their own abortions, but I never thought we would go back to the days when abortion was forbidden. I assumed, despite the protests and pro-life rhetoric, that abortion would remain a safe and legal medical procedure, not a moral issue based upon one religion's teachings. I had hoped people would realize that "Pro-Choice" does not always mean "Pro-Abortion": a woman can believe that abortion is not the right choice for her, yet still respect the right of other women to choose differently. But I was wrong.

The post-Roe world is disheartening and scary, yet not without hope. It is disheartening to see young women proclaiming that they are "The Post-Roe" generation and protesting against legal abortion. It is frightening that a small group of radical conservatives, including members of SCOTUS, took away the right to safe legal abortions for millions of people. Yet hope exists. SCOTUS's decision has enraged and empowered people who believe that abortion is a decision best left to women and their doctors. Women's clinics in Illinois stand up call centers to help women make arrangements to travel from far away states for abortions. Grant programs work to fund abortion—and travel—for women. And religious and civil rights groups file lawsuits to stop the radical right's war on women.

Despite the overturning of Roe, I am still hopeful that a woman's right to choose will ultimately prevail.

References

Bennett, G. (2014). *Abortion: Whose Religious Views Should Prevail.* Retrieved from *Huff Post.*

Bentele, K. G., Sager, R., & Aykanian, A. (2018). Rewinding Roe v. Wade: Understanding the Accelerated Adoption of State-Level Restrictive Abortion Legislation, 2018-2014. *Journal of Women, Politics & Policy*, 490-517.

Bray, B. (2008). *When Abortion Emotions Need Unpacking.* Retrieved from *Counseling Today.*

Geela, R. R. (n.d.). *Abortion Ritual.* Retrieved from RitualWell: https://www.ritualwell.org/ritual/abortion-ritual

Guttmacher Institute. (2019, April 1). *https://www.guttmacher.org/state-policy/explore/overview-abortion-laws.*

Retrieved from Guttmacher Institute: https://www.guttmacher.org/state-policy/explore/overview-abortion-laws

Jelen, T. G. (1992). The Clergy and Abortion. *Review of Religous Research*, 132-151.

LaFleur, W. R. (1990, October). Contestation and Consensus: The Morality of Abortion in Japan. *Philosophy East and West*, 529-542.

LaFleur, W. R. (1992). *Liquid LIfe: Abortion and Buddhism in Japan.* Princeton: Princeton University Press.

Malbon, C. C. (2012). *Abortion in the 21st Century.* North Charleston: CreateSpace Independent Publishing Platform.

Miyazaki, M. (2007). The history of abortion-related acts and current issues in Japan. *Medicine and Law*, 791-800.

NARAL Pro Choice America. (n.d.). *Fake Health Clinics.* Retrieved from Naral Pro Choice America:

National Abortion Federation. (n.d.). *History of Abortion.* Retrieved from National Abortion Federation: https://prochoice.org/education-and-advocacy/about-abortion/history-of-abortion/

Prichep, D. (2015). *Adopting A Buddhist Ritual To Mourn Miscarriage, Abortion.* Retrieved from National Public Radio.

Smith, B. (1988). Buddhism and Abortion in Contemporary Japan: "Mizuko Kuyo" and the Confrontation with Death. *Japanese Journal of Religous Studies*, 3-24.

Spruill, M. J. (2017). *Divided We Stand: The Battle over Women's Rights and Family Values that Polarized American Politics.* New York: Bloomsbury.

Nemesis

Kat Shaw

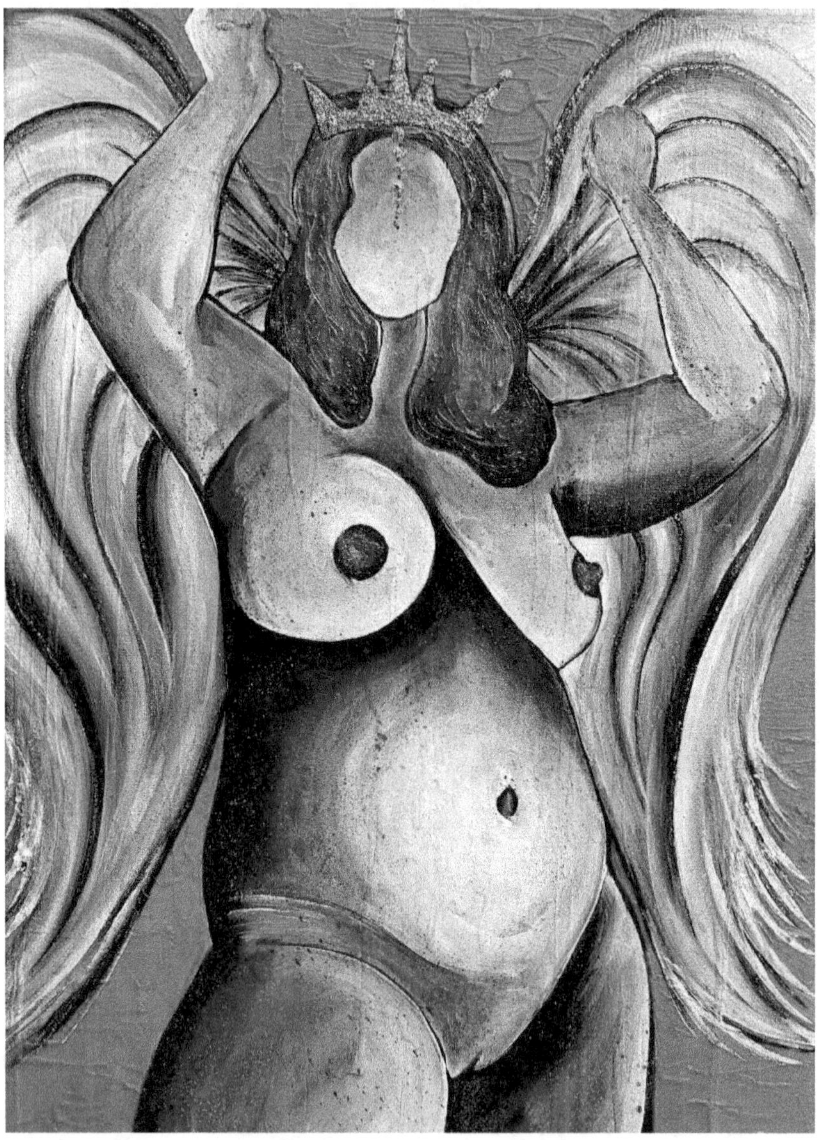

The Ancient Greek goddess who personifies retribution and sacred rage...
whose voice is heard in her anger at the injustice of the world...
She who screams aloud at the men who commit crimes against women...
She who restores the balance between good and evil...

Resist

Janis Ian

She is. She is. She is.
She is. She is. She is
She is. She is. She is
too short too fat too skinny
Too tall too plain too pretty
Too hot too wet too sticky
Too... picky
Oh, what an ugly girl. Oh, what an ugly girl.

Put her in high heels, so she can't run
Carve out between her legs so she can't come
Get her a dress, for easy access
Tell everybody that she's just like all the rest

How long? How long, how long, how long
How long? How long, how long, how long

Tell me I'm ugly so I'll buy your crap
Tell me you want me 'cause I don't talk back
Tell me I carry the original sin
Tell me I'm holy when I cover up my skin

Tell me that my body bears a permanent stain
Tell me we can marry if I give up my name
Call me your baby so I never grow up
Tell me you love me when you only want to fu-fu-fu-

Funny how I whisper and you think it's a roar
You ask me to the table then you seat me on the floor
You want me to be sexy. You want me to be pure.
I cannot be your virgin and I will not be your whore.

Resist. Resist resist resist.
Resist. Resist resist resist.

It's a funny kind of thing, when you sing a little song
and you get a couple people to sing along
It's the power of community.
Authenticity changes your reality
I know it's hard to believe when they're yelling in your ear
and it's the only voice you're able to hear
But you raise up your fist and you learn to resist
and you say "I will not disappear"
I will not disappear. I will not disappear.
I will not disappear, I will not disappear.
I will not disappear.

Resist. Resist resist resist.
Resist. Resist resist resist.
Resist, resist, resist. Resist, resist, resist, resist
Resist.

Pap Smears I Have Known

Molly Remer

"Your body is your own. This may seem obvious. But to inhabit your physical self fully, with no apology, is a true act of power."

–Camille Maurine (*Meditation Secrets for Women*)

*"I used to have fantasies... about women in a state of revolution.
I saw them getting up out of their beds and refusing the
knife, refusing to be tied down, refusing to submit... Women's health
care will not improve until women reject the present system
and begin instead to develop less destructive means of creating
and maintaining a state of wellness."*

–Dr. Michelle Harrison *(A Woman in Residence)*

One afternoon at the skating rink for homeschool playgroup, a few of my friends sit in a hard plastic booth and the conversation turns to pap smears and pelvic exams. Later, I read Michele Freyhauf's post about her hysterectomy experience and the skating rink pap smear stories come back to me with vivid clarity. Being a woman is such an *embodied experience* and we have so many stories to tell through and of our bodies. During my conversation with my friends, I warn them: watch for my new show – *Pap Smears I Have Known*. At the time, several other friends are preparing for a local production of the *Vagina Monologues* and I have a vision: *The Pap Smear Diaries*. But, really, how often do we have a chance to tell our Pap smear stories, our pelvic exam stories? Where are they in our culture and do they matter?

Three experiences come to mind as I talk with my friends...

1999. I am married, twenty years old, and a graduate student. I go to the student health center for my annual exam. As I walk up to the door and place my hand on the handle, I feel this intense, visceral reaction in my body of wanting to *run away*. For a few moments, I can't open the door, instead I think only of fleeing. The thought comes to me: I'm going in here to volunteer to be assaulted. Having to undergo a routine pelvic exam and pap smear as a condition of having access to birth control pills feels like a routine humiliation, like a ritual of physical invasion and "punishment" designed to shame young women who dare to have sex.

This is MY BODY.

2003. In my Type-A way, I head to a doctor for a "preconception visit" before my husband and I begin to try to conceive our first baby. This appointment is at a birth center in which you wear flowery housegowns instead of paper dresses. When the doctor touches me (she asks permission first), I flinch and recoil slightly. She looks at me with surprise: "Haven't you ever had a pap smear before?" I am intensely embarrassed because I know what she is thinking. She is thinking I must have been sexually abused and she is probably writing that on my chart right now. I haven't been sexually abused, though I've spent my formative late teens and early twenties working in domestic violence and sexual assault centers. I'm not sure why this feels so embarrassing to me, and I also still wonder, isn't it actually more normal to flinch when a stranger pushes their hand into your body than to be totally cool with it? Later at this birth center, I give birth to my first son. In what will eventually be six pregnancies, I only experience a single pelvic exam *ever* while pregnant, during his birth immediately before pushing. This is good. I prefer hands kept outside my body. After his birth, clots form in my uterus and prevent it from clamping down properly. The doctor does a manual exploration of my uterus to remove the clots. I scream out at first with the pain of this invasion and then hum my *Woman Am I* blessingway chant in order to cope.

This is MY UTERUS.

2009. My third baby has died unexpectedly during my second trimester. I give birth to him at home alone with just my husband. The baby's birth is surprisingly peaceful and empowering, but then the clots come, eventually the size of grapefruits. When I become unable to distinguish whether I am fainting from the unbelievable sight of *so much blood* or **dying** from the loss of it, I ask to go to the emergency room. The ER doctor tries to examine me to see if I am hemorrhaging, but she only has a child-sized speculum. She is unable to get her hand inside me because of the clots in the way. She puts the miniature speculum in over and over and it keeps flopping out because it is too small for me. I have never been so miserable. "This wouldn't hurt so much if you'd stop moving around so much," she says in an irritated voice. When she leaves the room, she leaves bloody handprints streaked along the sides of the bed and my blood in a puddle on the floor.

This is MY BLOOD.

> *"...no woman is powerful, no woman has 'come a long way baby'*
> *when she's made into medical mincemeat when giving birth. No*
> *woman is powerful when she lies on her back and flops her knees*
> *open for stranger's fingers and casual observation."*
>
> –Leilah McCracken, *Desexualizing Childbirth,* quoted in *Birthdance,*
> *Earthdance,* master's thesis by Nané Jordan (p. 58)

This February, I attend the local production of *The Vagina Monologues* performed by several of my friends before an encouragingly full theater in our small Midwestern town. One of them delivers a powerful portrayal of "My Angry Vagina." She is amazing and intense and angry as she stomps across the stage:

"...why the steel stirrups, the mean cold duck lips they shove inside you? What's that? My vagina's angry about those visits... Don't you hate that? 'Scoot down. Relax your vagina.' Why? So you can shove mean cold duck lips inside it. I don't think so. Why can't they find some nice delicious purple velvet and wrap it around me, lay me down on some feathery cotton spread, put on some nice friendly pink or blue gloves, and rest my feet in some fur covered stirrups?"

During my pregnancy with my daughter three years ago, I buy urinalysis strips on the internet and keep track of the protein, sugar, and leukocytes level in my urine. I monitor my blood pressure in the pharmacy section of the grocery store. I buy a Doppler and check her heartbeat myself. When I find myself continually worried about what I will do if she is not breathing at birth, I travel to a city several hours away and become certified in neonatal resuscitation. I buy a neonatal resuscitation bag and show my husband and mother how to use it. After she is born, breathing well, in wild, sweet relief into my own hands in my living room, I drink liquid chlorophyll to rebuild my blood supply and I ingest my own placenta dehydrated in little capsules prepared by my doula.

An acquaintance comes to me complaining that her insurance company does not cover her prenatal visits and she is tired of paying more than $100 for a five-minute visit while they check her urine and the baby's heartbeat. I feel a little nervous about it, but I pass her my Doppler and my leftover urinalysis test strips on the front porch of my little UU church. Later, she tells me how empowering it is to take care of these responsibilities herself, rather than going to the doctor for something she is perfectly capable of doing. Another friend borrows my Doppler several times to check heartbeats for other friends—sometimes with good news and sometimes with bad news—and in January of this year I have the honor and privilege of finding my brother and sister-in-law's first baby's heartbeat for the first time.

My friend asks to borrow my neonatal resuscitation equipment in case she needs it for a birth she is attending (it has already been to several other friends' houses during their births). I tell her, "I love black-market health care," and pass it to her furtively at the bowling alley.

Later, I reflect that it isn't black-market healthcare that I love, it is women taking care of each other and themselves. I love empowered self-care. I love *feminist* healthcare, though it has yet to exist on a systemic level in this country, and I love the possibility and potential found in taking the care of our bodies into our own hands whenever we can.

I have yet to invest in any speculums, but maybe I should. And, purple velvet.

Originally published on *Feminism and Religion* in 2014.

We Know How to Fly

Molly Remer

They have come for us
for generations,
bearing shackles and torches
and holy books that bind.
They have come for the midwives,
the wise women,
the priestesses,
and healers.
They have burned temples
and toppled statues
and stepped all over the sacred.
They have come for our bodies,
for our songs and our stories,
for our power and our pride.
Somehow they always forget
that no matter how many chains
they craft,
we are witches
and we know how to fly.

Tradition

Julia Jeffrey

Never Again: The Ancestors Speak

Arlene Bailey

They hover just on
the other side of the Veil,
waiting,
watching.

These women who
gave their lives
at the hands of Patriarchy
and its fear of
women's ways,
women's wisdom,
women's bodily functions.

They wait, these Ancestors,
watching the women of today
as they declare NEVER AGAIN!

They wait, as they work from
beyond the Veil to destroy
the Institution of Patriarchy,
responsible for Centuries
of continued murder and
subjugation of women.

ALL so I... We...
may clear the shi*t dumped
on EVERY WOMAN for the
past 6000 plus years.

They come...
They wait...
They question...

Will I step into my life's work
or take the easy way out and
do nothing?

They come...
They wait...
Asking if YOU will step into
Your life's work
OR
will you do nothing?

We stand on the precipice of
unfathomable shift in modern
times and the question is
which way will that shift go?

Will we do our part
or will we dull our senses
and trick our minds
into thinking and feeling
that the horror that lurks
on the horizon is only
in our imaginations?

Will we choose to hide
in illusion, while we go back
to numbing and dumbing down
the truth of our innate wisdom,
until the day...

Until the day we realize
the unfathomable
is no longer a theory,
but our reality,
as once again
the ancient and religious
Chains of Patriarchy

Reign Supreme and
women are once again
mere chattel to be
shackled and controlled.

They hover just beyond
the Veil waiting, watching.

These women who gave their lives
at the hands of Patriarchy
and its fear of
women's ways,
women's wisdom,
women's bodily functions,
women's body autonomy.

They wait, these Ancestors,
watching the women of today
as they declare NEVER AGAIN!

They wait, as they work from the
Realm of the Ancestors
to destroy Patriarchal Institutions
responsible for the Centuries
of continued murder and
subjugation of women.

They watch.
They wait.
They ask...

WILL we step into
our life's work?
OR
Will we do nothing as
we hide in denial?

Will we stand with
other women Even If
the decisions coming
down Do Not affect us?

We still have a choice...
But...
For How Long?

Dark Moon Blues

Dee Mulrooney

On Womanrage: How to Channel Your Anger in the Wake of the Reversal of Roe v. Wade

Sharon Smith

"What's wrong with you! Don't you know how crazy you sound?"

"Oh, Sister…I'm worried about you: That outburst is so low-vibe! You need to stop being angry and ask for a Spirit of Love to fill you!"

Anger and pain – even well-placed rage – has its purpose, and we must be careful not to shame or blame those who feel such strong emotions. I've felt them recently, felt them deeply, in the wake of the Supreme Court's decision to overturn Roe v. Wade.

It is human to feel. And, we don't always feel the "happy" feelings, do we?

For years I kept my so-called "negative" feelings (like anger and rage) deeply restrained within me. I thought it was the right thing to do. I wanted everyone to like me—and who likes an angry person, right? So I felt I had to put on a "happy face" or a "kind, loving face" all the time.

I smiled… but I hurt. And stuffing down my anger and rage caused stomach problems and restless, sleepless nights. I started popping Tums and then Prilosec to try to stop the acid reflux. All because I felt I couldn't be angry; I couldn't show rage.

It was like putting a lid on a boiling pot, but leaving no avenue for the steam to escape. It caused me to "blow my lid" from time to time… and then I felt shame and guilt for doing so.

It's never good to pretend you don't feel what you feel; and it's never healthy to try to mold yourself into some neat little package of "acceptability" so that you don't "offend" others.

It took me decades to learn that lesson, and it's only been a few years now that I've even given myself permission to be angry.

Since Roe v. Wade was done away with, I have felt the amalgamation of my suppressed anger and rage at all that is happening in our country concerning the stripping away of women's bodily autonomy... and I wanted to scream it all out.

But Goddess said to me, recently, in Her soothing Mama voice, "Daughter, do you trust Me?" I did not answer right away, contemplating why She was asking me that question. Then again, "Do you trust Me?" No booming, judgmental voice. Simply a profoundly caring one. "Yes... Yes I do!" I answered. "Then wait...and be patient." She said.

It was difficult that day, but I managed to wait. The next morning, however, Mama said to me: "Release your Womanrage. Don't hold back. It's time to honor it and give it a Voice."

It was very hard for me to do – far easier, it would have been, to go out into the woods and scream that rage to the trees. But I did as She said, knowing full well there would be friends and possibly even family members who would be shocked and perhaps even offended by my rage (not to mention my use of "expletives" that underscored that rage) at the current anti-abortion legislation cropping up in "red states" around the country.

I felt like a volcano erupting, spewing forth a pyroclastic cloud of "F" words... or a wildfire unrestrained, leaving the ground blackened in its wake. And that was when Mama helped me see that Womanrage is very much a potent force of Nature. She told me, "Volcanoes gotta blow, and the Earth's gotta quake... and a Woman's gotta rage when she has to!"

So, I channeled my rage where it needed to go: at Patriarchy and the people who keep this destructive Dominator System going. People like Donald Trump, Mitch McConnell, Matt Gaetz, Todd Rokita, and the Supreme Court justices who threw out an almost 50-year-old ruling in favor of women's bodily autonomy, something our ancestral mothers and grandmothers had fought, suffered and even died for.

I aimed that rage right at them. I was not "Love & Light." I was Tooth & Claw, like a Mama Bear protecting her cubs. I sliced, diced and shredded without apology. And I did it in the way I know best: through speaking, and through my writing.

And, you know what? It felt good! It was deeply cathartic.

As Soraya Chemaly says in her book, *Rage Becomes Her: The Power of Women's Anger:*

> *"Ask yourself, why would a society deny girls and women, from cradle to grave, the right to feel, express, and leverage anger and be respected when we do? Anger has a bad rap, but it is actually one of the most hopeful and forward thinking of all our emotions. It begets transformation, manifesting our passion and keeping us invested in the world. It is a rational and emotional response to trespass, violation, and moral disorder. It bridges the divide between what 'is' and what 'ought' to be, between a difficult past and an improved possibility. Anger warns us viscerally of violation, threat, and insult."*

We've been violated in this country under patriarchal institutions – as women, as men, as Human Beings. I think it's safe to say most of us feel it deeply, in our blood... in our bones. But few of us (myself included) have had the courage to admit we rage inwardly... and want to let that rage out. I denied it for years.

But I can't, and I won't, deny it any longer.

And so, that day not long ago, I took a leap of faith and "let it all hang out".

As one Sister, whom I deeply respect (for she is a true Wise Woman) said to me about a woman's rage: "*If not now, then when? If not us, then who?*"

Women inherently know how to handle rage. Yes, we've been told otherwise and many have been led to believe that Womanrage makes a woman "crazy", "incapacitated" and "unlikeable".

But we know… At the core of our beings, we know that is not true.

Our Womanrage actually helps to keep us sane. It is an emotional pressure valve within us that we must turn every now and then to allow the emotion of anger to vent, so that our internal Yin/Yang of Light/Dark energies remains balanced. If we suppress it, it will eventually overload, and when that happens… watch out! That's when "Crazy" shows up!

Womanrage, properly understood and wisely channeled, is a tremendously creative force. Just like a volcanic flow (which is scary as hell when it's happening) or a raging wildfire (note: also scary as hell) are destructive forces of Mama Nature, they are also creative forces as well: New growth happens soon after they blacken the earth. So, too, with Womanrage. It can totally shred to pieces injustices and level to the ground social systems, rooted and grounded in religious, political and economic disparities. But in its wake, it leaves fertile soil in which new and better ideas and solutions take shape and are born.

So, beware when people tell you that your anger, your rage, is "negative" and "low vibe": it's not. Beware when they chasten you and try to make you feel bad for it: don't internalize undeserved shame. Don't allow others to gaslight you with the "Love & Light" shame & blame game. Love & Light are all good, and we do need them. But as a very wise Indigenous Grandmother once told me:

"Light can blind you and render you incapable of truly seeing. Too much of it is not good! As the Day needs the Night; as the Sun needs the Moon, so too, we need the Dark to balance the Light."

I have never forgotten those words. And through my subsequent time in the School of the Dark Goddess (Thank you, Hecate and The Morrigan!), I have come to understand more clearly my own inner Darkness, and to honor and embrace it—and use it, when necessary, for it is a place of Strength and Courage, the Realm of the Kick-Ass Warrior Woman (just ask Lilith sometime).

I raged. It wasn't pretty. But as I said, it was deeply cathartic. And when it was over, when the wildfire had burned itself out, I felt in those crackling embers new thoughts, new ideas, ready to spark. (I even got a great idea for a novel out of it!)

Afterwards, I felt refreshed, invigorated, cleansed. Maybe *purged* is a better word. I purged a lot of anger from my Womansoul. And while some might not see how any of my "rantings" could be productive, I know what they did for me.

My rage is mine. It's not yours. It's not anyone else's. It's mine. And it has to work for me.

But here's the thing about Womanrage. Although our rage is unique to each of us, we, as women, share so many similar "rage triggers" that together our combined rage—again, channeled properly (we mustn't allow ourselves to detonate prematurely)—is a nearly unstoppable force for positive change. And if we ever needed positive changes, it's now.

So, honor your Womanrage. Get to know it. Sit with it. Listen to it. Embrace it. And when the time is right, give it a voice. Let your Womanrage work for you as a source of creativity. Write it out (spew those words onto paper, if you need to!), dance it out, sing it out, bang it out on a drum, pound it out in clay, splash it out in color onto paper or canvas… Speak it, to the Cosmos if you have to (Mama will listen!).

Believe me, Sisters, in these dark times when we're fighting for our sovereignty against an onslaught of patriarchal politics and religion, you will be all the better for it.

Cailleach

Dee Mulrooney

Foremothers

Arlene Bailey

I feel like a dinosaur
So out of place in this time
I'm tired and I'm ancient
And feel as though there is
A target on my body
Just because I am an old woman
Just because I am not the
Male of the species nor the
Nubile of mine they so crave

I am no longer essential
Even though I am THE portal
Through which ALL human
Life comes,

BUT...

I cannot create that life
Alone and the male of the
Species feels he has no
Responsibility other than
Using me as a depository
For his semen – you know
His "part" in creation of
A child

As for younger women, it
Would appear they are
A holding place and that
NOTHING else about them
Matters other than their uterus
Which fucking men want to
Use, Abuse and Control

Sure, there are good men out there
Who do not feel this way, but they
Are the minority and, with rare
Exception, where are they when
It comes to protests and protection
Of me and any potential child that
Might be created

No. I am female and the definition of
That should be "She Who Exists Alone"
Or perhaps, more accurately,
"She Who Exists only for the pleasure of Men"
For they care not for any child that
May result from the taking of their
Pleasure whenever, wherever and
However they deem appropriate

Yes. A dinosaur that like my sisters
Of old were accused of all sorts of
Things and subjected to the most
Horrific atrocities. In the minds of
Men, I have outlived my usefulness
As I can no longer birth a child
And am no longer young and innocent.
I know too much. See too much.
Have skills that can instill fear in
The "bravest" of them

Bravest – Ha!

Now that's a moniker that is outdated
When it comes to the male of the species.
He rules not by bravery, but by control,
Brute force and instilling fear

He rules by seeking out the most ancient,
Restrictive laws on women and bringing
It/them forward into this time.
He cares not for me or any woman
Not for babies or children

Not for any damn thing but the
dangly thing that hangs limp
between his legs and the freedom
to use it when and as he pleases

And

Damn the consequences for
Any woman or child in his path

Our Lady of the Shadows

Dee Mulrooney

The Right to Privacy

Deborah A. Meyerriecks

The word 'woman' occurs exactly zero times in the United States Constitution.

The word freedom is also absent.

There is over a century of precedent against women doing anything out of the gender role assigned to them by a male dominated society in the highest court of law in the United States, the Supreme Court.

It's important to note that Roe v. Wade is about much more than the right to access an abortion by choice. It solidified and expanded the constitutional "right to privacy," which has also been described as the right to autonomy or to be let alone as set forth in the 14th Amendment.

The primary reason Congress enacted the 14th Amendment to the US Constitution was to place limits on an individual state's power and to protect the civil rights of US citizens. Some southern states were passing laws that restricted the rights of former slaves after the Civil War. Congress responded with the 14th Amendment.

Don't want to have an abortion? Then don't have one. This goes deeper than a woman's right to choose what happens to and with her own body.

The 14th Amendment has 3 main sections:

- The amendment's first section focuses on citizenship and civil liberties and includes several clauses: the Citizenship Clause, Privileges or Immunities Clause, Due Process Clause, and Equal Protection Clause.

- The second section addresses Apportionment of Representatives. It was intended to penalize, by means of reduced Congressional representation, states that withheld the franchise from adult male citizens for any reason other than participation in crime. (Notice, specifically male citizens only are afforded protection.) It details enforcement and influence on voting rights. (Again, specifically to men and not women).

    - Also important to note is that the 2nd clause of the 14th amendment is the first time women were not just absent from the constitution, it protects the right to vote only of adult males, not adult females, making it the only provision of the Constitution to explicitly discriminate on the basis of sex. (A precedent that has been built on time and time again.)

- The third section specifies the disqualification from office for insurrection or rebellion. While being arrested and charged with and even convicted of some crimes will not bar an individual from being able to hold an elected office within the US government, the third clause of the 14th amendment legalized a specific consequence of insurrection and rebellion against the existing US government. I mean, it makes sense, right? And I would think that the individual(s) who participated in an insurrection or rebellion wouldn't be looking to work within the existing governmental body but looking for another way to dismantle it from within.

- Section four covers the validity of public debt. We see this in modern times when a sitting president enacts the 14th Amendment to validate raising the US' Debt Ceiling, which in turn will financially affect everyone in the country.

- Section five, also known as the Enforcement Clause of the Fourteenth Amendment, enables Congress to pass laws enforcing the amendment's other provisions. It is the authoritative power behind the laws created that by

"Whatever legislation is appropriate, that is, adapted to carry out the objects the amendments have in view, whatever tends to enforce submission to the prohibitions they contain, and to secure to all persons the enjoyment of perfect equality of civil rights and the equal protection of the laws against State denial or invasion, if not prohibited, is brought within the domain of congressional power." (excerpted from *Encyclopedia of the American Constitution*)

The right to privacy stems from the right to liberty which is protected under both the 5th and 14 amendments. We as citizens are guaranteed the right and shall not be deprived of "life, liberty or property, without due process of law."

While the Constitutional right to privacy is older than Roe v. Wade, Roe v. Wade confirmed it as a fundamental right as it relates to contraception and procreation, marriage, family relations, child rearing, and intimacy.

Privacy related to each of these areas were influenced and confirmed by Roe v. Wade and now that the US Supreme Court has overturned their ruling on Roe v. Wade, it's a valid concern that other individual rights under the right to privacy will come under attack.

From an individual's personal choice as to whether or not they wish to bear children to the right to marry whomever they want to marry who also wants to marry them regardless of ethnicity or gender. The very personal right to intimacy between consenting adults in the manner they choose to share said intimacy. Not only was the right to decide whether or not to have a child previously protected, the same law that issued the right to choice protected the right to make decisions regarding how one's own child would be raised. Maybe that one will get some people's attention.

What do I mean? Losing the individual right to decide how you will raise your own child means losing the right to keep your child home with you if you don't follow the new laws when this one is revoked. Not only not having any say over what and how they are taught or exposed to while at school, losing the right to homeschool if you saw fit to do so for your family. Never forget the horror of our government's Indian Boarding Schools.

Finally, the right to personal control of medical treatment is at risk. Privacy covers your medical conditions, treatment, and your decisions about that treatment. Whether you are pro-vaccines, anti-vaccines, (or any medication or treatment,) or simply are feeling skepticism and want more information and time to be able to come to an informed decision, your right to privacy and the right to personal control of medical treatment is protected under the 14th Amendment and now is on the same shaky ground as the personal choice to abort an unwanted or unsafe pregnancy and interracial or same sex marriage. Remember the experimental medical testing that was done with detrimental effect to marginalized communities of people who conveniently didn't fall under the protection of our constitution.

Be aware that the right to generate a healthcare proxy to establish which medical treatments you would consent to and which you would deem personally unwanted and wish to refuse has only existed since 1990 because the Supreme Court voted it in based on the precedent set by Roe v. Wade and the liberty interest doctrine.

The word 'woman' does not appear in the US Constitution. Nor does the word 'freedom.'

Women are not livestock to be bred and discarded. I read that to some, a baby is a gift while the mother is simply just the wrapping and packaging that delivered it. To be discarded. And the child too will be discarded by society at large soon after the novelty and newness have worn away.

People should have the inalienable right to decide what does or does not happen to their bodies. Without a verified organ donor status, we cannot take lifesaving organs or tissue from a corpse. Without the legal documentation to verify the recently dead wished for it, you cannot cremate a corpse and it must be buried intact.

A corpse has more rights and body autonomy than a woman.

I thought we were finally progressing towards a healthy society where we could simply say a person, people, a citizen, the citizens. No categorizational adjective where we are separated by race and/or gender. Marriage, any marriage between consenting adults regardless of race or gender is simply a marriage. I still hear the prefix "Lady" used before her job title. "Lady" doctor, "Female" mechanic.

I have a friend who is a respected research author who has been told at conferences that 'she' doesn't know what 'she' is speaking about – and is then told to read books by experts in the field only to have their own books recommended to them. To add to the disrespect, they are non-binary and their pronouns are they/them. They typically dress gender-neutral and assuming the majority of people don't personally know them, they include it in their personal greeting/introduction before speaking. Some people see a woman and immediately disregard anything they say. I have seen it first-hand.

A woman, who wants sex but not to have a baby, is told she shouldn't have had sex if she conceives. No one tells the man they should have remained abstinent until he wanted to be a father. If a woman is raped she's victimized again if she is brave enough to tell. If that rape resulted in conception, she's told to deal with it (but not by having an abortion). All the while, it's been abundantly clear that restricting legal and safe access to abortion was never the end goal. Merely a stepping stone.

Am I mad? I'm furious. We are supposed to leave the world better for our children and the next generation. Many native and indigenous cultures take it several steps further. The Seven Generation Principle teaches that every action and decision one makes should take into consideration its impact on the next seven generations while at the same time, taking into consideration the lessons learned by the previous seven generations.

I know it feels like the people who pushed to overturn Roe v. Wade, rather than work to bolster the 14th amendment's protections and rights granted though Roe v. Wade, by adding more case study and precedent, are laying the groundwork towards other reversals. I worry for the generations to come as much as I worry for the ones still here. I worry that rather than continuing to progress into equality we are regressing back to where we came from, which was not very long ago.

Freedom may not be a word used in the entirety of the US Constitution, yet it is a fundamental principle our nation was founded on. It's the principle we celebrate every 4th of July. Relative to today, the question we need answered is: freedom for or from what and who?

My Body. My Rights.

Reverend Rebecca M. Bryan

I am the seven-year-old girl who lost her saddle shoe running the Presidential Youth Fitness Test and walked the last part of the mile around the outdoor track, alone with the pine trees to witness my finish.

I am the young woman in her 20s who bore children and did kickboxing and step aerobics until my insides felt like they were coming out. No one, not even I, understood why I ran so hard.

I am the 40-year-old woman coming into her truth saying, "This happened." The 40-year-old who ran a half marathon for the younger parts of herself, with chosen sisters there to cheer her on. I am not alone. I am not crazy.

Today, I am the 56-year-old woman, dancing and singing my heart out to music that makes me smile, running on a treadmill that reads 4.7 mph.

I know the race is over, and the walk of reclaiming my innocence, my truth, and my voice, continues.

I am a woman in charge of her story, her body, and her destiny.
A woman that everyone has the right to be.

#WomensBodiesWomensRights

Great Cosmic Mother

Arlene Bailey

Her Lament

Arlene Bailey

Where is the darkness that will hold me,
that which will shield me from the
destruction of man?

Oh that I could reach back in space and time
to the beginning when women were seen
as powerful, revered, sacrosanct, sovereign.

Instead, this Now makes me long for the
watery depths of nothingness...
Nothing more than The Mother holding me,
caressing my tears and shushing my cries.

What is it to walk in this time of man?
This time when they speak of Not being
responsible, Not needing to do this or that
and yet, Demanding servitude and submission
to the ways of the Father, the Husband, the
F^~king God-Damned Patriarchal Religion
permeating every aspect of society!

I long for another time and yet I was born
to this one... this inane and insane point in
time and space allowing for nothingness...
No-thing-ness and, yet, the potential for
everything... all things yet to be born
held in time and space waiting to be
called forward by a woman, but only a
woman of this time, in this place, in this
vast space of a universe that births us all.

But who will answer such a call knowing
that which awaits?

Burkhas and Clitoridectomies!
Forced pregnancies and poverty!
Rape, Molestation and even death!

Sex Trafficking and imprisonment under
the guise of protecting a woman's virtue!

The horrors of the insatiable, perverted
appetites of the male of the species as
Abortion Rights are thrown into the flames
of the fire that also burned the witches,
wise women, elder women along with
men, children and animals.

Who would answer such a call
to This time, This place, These ways ?
Who would knowingly and willingly
answer a call to walk as a woman
in this time knowing what awaits?

And...

Who would dare NOT answer these calls,
for the future of Earth and ALL her children
depends on women answering this call.
Our very future as free, independent women
demands we answer this call as does the
future of generations of women still to come!

For it takes one who knows the Mysteries
One able to create, birth and sustain life and
One to end life in All the ways women do this
to understand that which is at stake and what
is required to lift us out of this time of man as
we Reclaim the Temple and Her ancient ways
of reverence and sustainability...
Her ancient ways held in sacred power.

Where is the darkness that will hold me,
teaching me the courageous, independent,
defiant choice of Lilith?

Where are the ways of the mysteries of
Hecate and Persephone, Erishkigal and Inanna
The Morrighan and Queen Boudicca, the
Great Mother Isis and the Rage of Kali?

The Mysteries and the ways which will allow
me to walk in this world of man while knowing
the rituals and ways that will strengthen that which
is to survive and subvert that which is to die?

Oh that I could reach back in space and time
to the beginning... to Lilith and her Serpent
standing in power as they demand and own
innate wisdom and mysteries known only to
the few who are wise enough, powerful enough
to say NO to the evils and weakness of man and
His sky god.

Oh that I could reach back in space and time
when women were seen as powerful, wise
sacrosanct, sovereign...

A time when they were revered as the
All of the All, the Both/And reflecting the
As Above, So Below in their very
knowings of all planes.

Where is the Darkness that holds me in birth,
in death and, perhaps most auspiciously,
in this very Now where it seems women
are nothing more than a body for men to
control and inhabit, nothing more than
a place where babies are forcibly born
only to become the playthings of sick,
aberrant, abhorrent men with insatiable
appetites for power over all things female.

Oh that I could reach back in space and time
surrounded by the presence of those wise women
whose images mark the walls in perpetuity,
where unseen forces surround me and hold me
connecting me to those wise foremothers.

As I hold my torch, so do others
As I remember, so do others
As I bow to the grace of woman's
Strength, power and wisdom
So do others.

I Am Not Free

Reda Rackley aka Bonewoman

I am not free
You want to control my body
to control my mystery!
You write your laws in the halls of the dead
Scraping my womb with your hate & dread.

I am not free
You say you will throw me in prison and throw away the key
If I choose what is right for me.

I am not free
You have taken away my sovereignty
brought me to my knees.
Now I pray to the Mothers of Liberty,

The wild ones, the uncontrollable ones,
The dark mothers who screech in the night
Who will never give up the fight
For the rights of women to decide their own fate.

I am not free
Fourth of July is just a lie
Been that way since them six white men wrote these words:
"We hold these truths to be self-evident, that all men are created
equal, that they are endowed by their Creator with certain
unalienable rights, that among these are Life, Liberty and the
Pursuit of Happiness."

Freedom was given to the old white men
Sacrificing BIPOC & women
in the name of their sin.

No, I am not free in the land of my county tis of thee
Sweet land of liberty
For all eternity
Let freedom ring
Let freedom ring

Mothers of Liberty

Reda Rackley aka Bonewoman

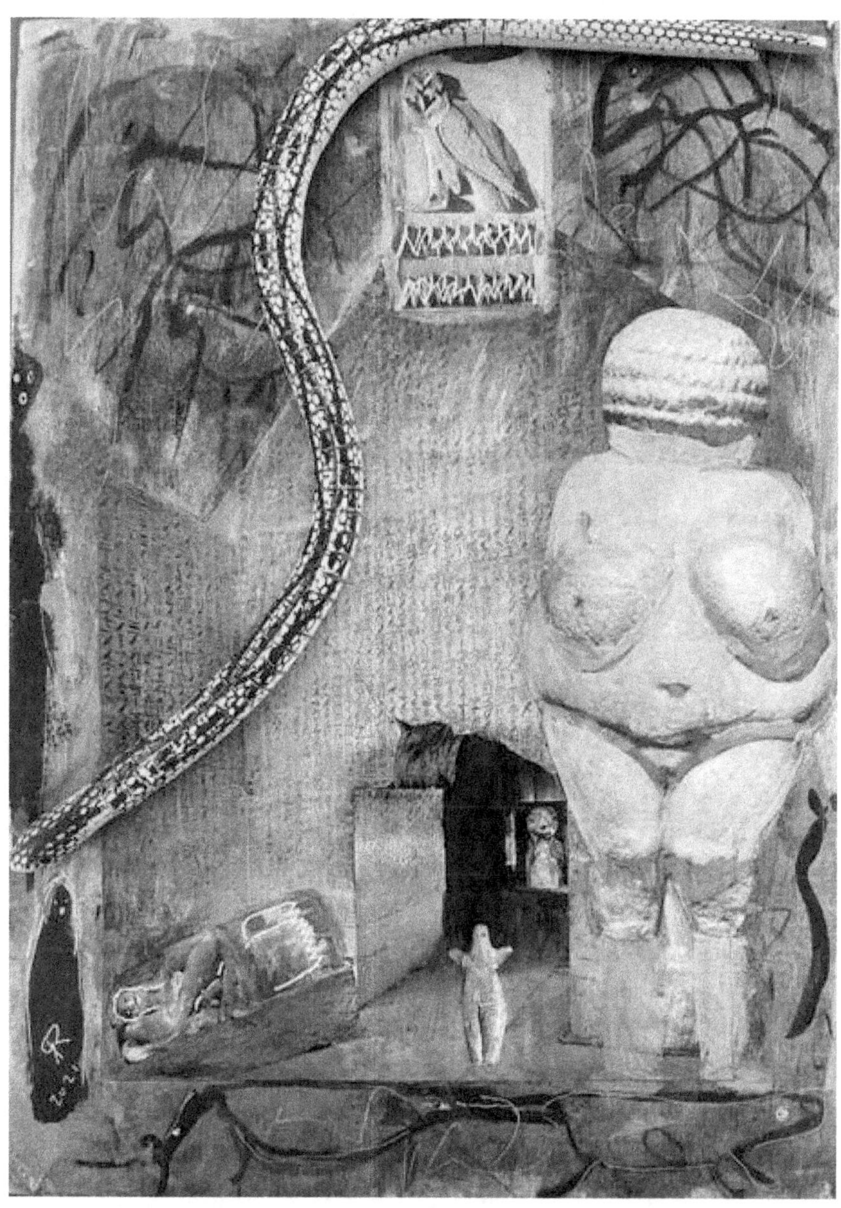

Swamp Woman

Reda Rackley aka Bonewoman

Old Swamp Woman lives down in the Bayou since the beginning of time. She's the original wise woman, powerful granny-witch. She can raise the dead and heal the living. She's a strong, big boned woman, the color of red mud her bare feet walk through. She loves the children and the children love her. She gives them sweets she made from the mint that grows down by the stream. She got no need for them menfolk, it's best they stay away. She loves love; she loves her some good loving from a woman every now and then, but don't want nobody hanging around too long. Everybody knows where to take their sisters, daughters, wives, if they need to end a pregnancy and they know Swamp Woman got the root medicines to get a woman with child. Swamp Woman places her powerful healing hands on a woman's womb and chants the old songs from the times the women gathered in the caves and left their handprints thousands of years ago. If a man ever harms a woman, she'll come looking for him in the disguise of a beautiful young woman and she'll feed him chocolate covered in poison, then throw him to the alligators. Old Swamp Woman loves her a little rum, cigars, a rooster every now and then; best to leave these offerings on the back porch.

ABORTION AS A SACRAMENT:
A POET'S PERSPECTIVE

Annie Finch

There is great insight in this feminist truism from the 1970s: "if men could get pregnant, abortion would be a sacrament." According to Faye Wattleton's memoir, this pithy remark was first spoken by a female cab driver as she drove Wattleton and Gloria Steinem to a feminist rally in New York City. We might think of the sacrament part of the quote as an ironic joke, an over-exaggeration for comedic effect. But I began to take the remark much more seriously after I had an abortion myself, as a 42-year-old witch and a mother of two, and encountered a profound spiritual depth in the experience. It was then that I finally came to understand the complex web of will, mind, body, heart, and spirit, of family, self, and society, of future and past, that may be summoned and considered and experienced in the choice to end a pregnancy.

By the time I had the abortion, I had considered the decision deeply and—for reasons I needn't go into here—was sure it was absolutely the right one for myself and our family. The procedure itself was smooth and painless, even beautiful. The doctor was experienced, gentle, and sensitive. The clinic was so aware of the spiritual and psychological dimensions of abortion that I was invited to choose a lovely smooth small stone to hold during the operation and bury afterwards to create closure. It would be hard to imagine a better abortion clinic experience.

That's why it totally blindsided me when I headed into a horrible depression soon afterwards. I'd wake up each morning with tears in my eyes and a lead weight on my heart as it sunk in yet again that I had ended a life inside me and that I was completely alone with this bitter awareness. Had I made the wrong decision after all? I went over and over it in my head, turned it over and over in my heart, but nothing changed. I felt paralyzed. It was as if I'd been poisoned. Much of the anger was against my husband. *He* didn't have to wake up every morning living with the knowledge that he had killed our baby inside his body. How could he go on living his life as if the whole thing were no big deal? The family in general, the world in general, everyone else just kept moving forward with their lives as if things were fine. What looked like their callousness and heedlessness was unbearable.

And so it went for the better part of a year, as I struggled to claim my power. Witchcraft is about making use of the fullness of our Goddess-given selves. It can be frightening to embrace our more shadowy forces: fear, anger, fury, death, and grief. But that work is just as essential as coming to love. The shadow, when embraced with compassion, has great gifts to offer us. In contrast with monotheistic ideas of perfect good and unacceptable evil, the Goddess of the witches embraces day and night, death and life in one. As a witch, I try to allow each of my feelings its place, even the fierce and destructive ones— to experience each energy as much as possible without judgment. A large part of my spiritual healing and growth has come from integrating those parts of myself that had been repressed or ignored. During those hard months after the abortion, I stretched myself in new ways, aiming to come to terms with the "hard Goddess" in me; like Coatlicue or Kali, I needed to put on my necklace of skulls.

One Saturday morning almost a year after the abortion, the hard Goddess's work with me was done. I woke up and instantly realized, in one crystal-clear instant, what my problem was. It was simple. I needed a post-abortion ritual. And it had to be a family ritual. The abortion had been a community decision—but I had been trying to handle all the spiritual work of processing and coming to terms with it completely alone. This literally wasn't possible because, though I had had the final say, the decision had *never* been made for my own sake alone. I had made it for my family as a whole. So, the hugely serious moment needed to be marked within the community that it affected—the community of our family. We needed a family ritual.

The ritual we used (which may be found in my epic poem about a sacred abortion, *Among the Goddesses*) was beautiful. Soon after we started the ceremony, a deer gave us the blessing of its company, watching us from a couple of feet away until we were finished. Afterwards we walked in silence through the woods, all four holding hands, connected with reverence for the gift of life, gratitude for each other, and grace in our humility at the endless depths we had navigated together. It was an amazing day.

The next morning, I woke up with a light heart for the first time since the abortion. My depression had vanished, and in the twenty years since the abortion, I have felt only peaceful, calm, and grateful. About four years after the abortion, during a yoga class at the Stone House in Freeport, Maine, I felt the soul of the baby leave me and move out into the trees. Since then, I have felt its spirit out in the universe as a beautiful spirit blessing me and smiling. (Recently, I came across a yogic teaching saying that it takes the soul of a baby four years to leave after an abortion).

Though becoming a witch has been a lifelong, gradual process during which I have enacted and developed many rituals, if I had to choose one moment to mark the time I entered my full witchy power, this would be it. This ritual was the first time in my life that I had been thrown entirely on my own resources as a witch, to craft a ritual that was necessary for my survival and that I had no idea how to obtain in any other way. With this ritual I saved my own life, both in a spiritual sense and on a more literal level, since living with such misery and anger would surely have debilitated me physically.

A friend who is a therapist tells me that she feels many of the women in her practice who are most troubled carry unresolved grief from abortions, and that therapy doesn't seem to be addressing it. I used to wonder why, as a person who has successfully used many kinds of therapy, I didn't seek out therapy after my abortion (although a fabulous book by a therapist, *Peace After Abortion*, truly was helpful). My sense of it now is that I was suffering, not from a wound within my separate self, but instead, from a more raw and basic need that had to be satisfied outside myself, with others: the simple hunger for the spiritual nurturing of communal ritual at one of the most profound moments of my life, the moment when I encountered not only the blood mystery of birth, not only the blood mystery of death, but both of them combined, together, at once.

I hope that my ritual here will be of help to others who are in the same position, and not only for individuals on the personal level, but also for women collectively, on the political level. I firmly believe that in order for us to claim our matricultural power once more and help the human species re-emerge from the death-cult of patriarchy, we will need to make complete peace with our power over life and death. We will need to disentangle our Goddess-given right to manage our own pregnancies from whatever guilt and shame patriarchal religion has tried to pile onto female bodies. We will need to reclaim female-centered spirituality, with its embrace of the physical world, reverence for the sensual, and understanding of the sacred aspects of both life and death. And we will need to embrace the power of ritual that women have always used to move ourselves spiritually and to make our mysteries whole.

The current abortion "debate," with its obsessing over certain circumstances (incest, rape, life of the mother, age of the fetus) that supposedly make abortion more "acceptable"— in the eyes of a patriarchal moral system based on a punitive, hierarchical monotheistic religion—is trying desperately to fill the spiritual vacuum. It would be funny if it weren't so tragic. Those who get stuck arguing about the morality of abortion based on "when life begins" are scared to face one indisputable fact: women have power over life and death. It comes with the territory. Abortion is always a life-death decision, however many weeks along. No matter when life begins, women have always and will always have powers to stop it. Period. (And speaking of periods, most women have been dealing with our power over life and death every month since puberty, and most of us, thank the Goddess, know how to use our power over life and death with love and with wisdom.)

Mainstream feminism—still shackled to the idea of monotheistic patriarchal religion as the only plausible spiritual path—has so far framed abortion rights strictly as a secular experience, forcing those who want to experience their abortions in spiritual terms to choose between a patriarchal religion's spiritual guilt or a strictly secular approach to the act of abortion. But there is a third way: a spiritual path centered on the Divine Feminine. Combining birth, love, and death, abortion is potentially as spiritual an experience as one could imagine. Because the Goddess encompasses both life and death (unlike the transcendent male God), the Goddess can provide a spiritual context for abortion without guilt, shame, or judgement. On the path of the witch and in the sight of the Goddess, as hinted at in my long-ago postcard, it truly is possible to experience a sacred approach to abortion.

On the page that follows is the poem I wrote to express my sense of abortion as a sacred act shared by mother and baby, in the sight of the Goddess.

AN ABORTION DAY SPELL FOR TWO VOICES

(To be spoken aloud three times:
One stanza for the mother,
one stanza for the baby,
and *one* for *both together.)*

As I turn your blood back to the earth.
I am life. You are death. And we kiss.
Through the fire that is my freedom's birth.

By the womb of our love's endlessness,
As you turn my blood back to the earth,
I am death, you are life. And we kiss

Till we move *through the deep,* giving forth
To the web of our love-woven bliss,
Through *the fire that is* our freedom's birth!

In My Womb

Dee Mulrooney

Body, Mind, Soul & Plants

Anna Begas

You can't stop the tides from rising

She is taken for granted
Expected to always be there
With her presence
Her care, her time, her body, her love, her attention,
her availability, her life
Expected to serve
Taken for granted

Her needs?
End of the list
They are not convenient
It is too easy to fall back into the arms of male superiority,
so let's just say
She is selfish
She is crazy
She is unstable
Too emotional to make clear decisions
Too needy
Yeah, if she gets very intense let's just call her lunatic, manic, crazy
It's easy, we have enough evidence to back this up

To support her?
And understand that that is supporting the whole family,
the whole village, the whole society?
No, that is not convenient at all
In fact, it is scary
When she is kept small, it feels quite good,
it makes us feel big and powerful
It feels we got it all under control
But what about that mystic dark wet power that we don't
understand
We can't grasp, we can't hold on to?

What if that gets unleashed?
The power that growls during childbirth
Her intimacy with life and death
Her boiling anger of being suppressed
Her orgasmic waves of pleasure
Her capacity to bring us into surrender

What if she gets unleashed?

We can't deal with that

It scares the shit out of us

It is too unknown. Too raw. Too far beyond. And we know it will bash down our pumped-up egos and that will hurt. We don't like pain. We haven't learnt how to breathe through the pain. How to die unto ourselves before the birth of new life. How to surrender our mind to the pulse of the Universe. How to surrender our opinions to the unknown forces of life. And we are too scared to do so.

So...
Let's continue to try to push her down,
until she bows down before us
Enslave her in her motherhood without support
Enslave her in her multitasking without acknowledgement
Enslave her in the objectification of her body
Enslave her within man-made laws that don't permit fluidity

But just remember that the tides are turning, and the tides are stronger than us all. And in those dark depths of the mystic ocean of the feminine, she is free and has always been free.
And she is wave after wave crashing on the shores.
You can't stop the tides rising.

Bodies

Rachael Noton

Don't Take it Lying Down

Kaalii Cargill

Why do law makers think they can decide a woman's reproductive choices?

The answers to that question take the recent Supreme Court decision to overturn Roe vs Wade into the bigger story of what has happened to women's mysteries throughout the ages and shifts our focus to true reproductive autonomy. I stand for abortion on demand as a legal right, and I also want women to claim true reproductive autonomy that is not dependent on anyone's permission. We are at the threshold of another revolution and have an opportunity to participate in what may be a crucial turning for the continuance of life on Earth. How each of us approaches this will impact on the Earth, the original matter… mater… mother of us all.

Reproductive autonomy has long been a particular focus of patriarchal law makers. Unrest, fear, and full-blown rage are appropriate responses to the Supreme Court decision. They are also appropriate responses to all patriarchal beliefs, attitudes and practices that deny power, choice, and control in women's lives.

Why has reproductive autonomy been such a focus? Because women have always been able to do something that men cannot do: grow and bring forth new life from our bodies. This life-giving power is so obvious that we forget the magic of it. Life does not come through men's bodies, test tubes, or incubators; life still comes into being through women's bodies. Despite contraceptive chemicals and more than three thousand years of negative conditioning, women's bodies continue to respond to the rhythms of Nature. That we tend to take this for granted (and even see it as a burden women must bear) represents a terrible loss of power. Whether or not we choose to have children, women are the life-givers. It is this life-giving power that church and state have worked to control for a long time.

Once upon a time, when "God was a woman"[4], anywhere from 35,000 years ago until about 3,500 years ago in some parts of the world, the life-giving power of Goddess was deeply respected. Consistent with this, women were respected as the life-givers, and the functions of pregnancy, birth, and nurturing were valued as reflections of Great Mother, the mother of all. The rhythms and cycles of Nature were honoured in ceremonies and rituals, in daily practices that reflected a reverence for Goddess. Over the last few thousand years, this has changed so that the world in which we now live has little of this respect and acknowledgement. These changes have resulted in the loss of ancient ways of knowing.

Women in some parts of the world did once know how to manage fertility in a simple, uncomplicated, internal way, with little need to use any outside devices, programs, or interventions. If these were needed, there is considerable evidence that simple, safe birth control was also available in the form of vaginal sponges, herbs and abortifacient drugs.[5]

This is a very different story from the official version of history which tells us that women were at the mercy of Nature during their childbearing years until the advent of the Contraceptive Pill. This other story tells of women's mysteries destroyed by church and state authorities and various individuals, all of whom were jealous and/or fearful of women's life-giving power. In this story there are social, religious and cultural factors that have deeply affected the way we think about ourselves, our bodies, and reproductive choices. The reversal of the Roe vs Wade decision is only the most recent example of this.

---

[4] M Stone, 1978, *When God Was a Woman*, New York, Harcourt Brace Jovanovich.
[5] G Davis, 1974, *Interception of Pregnancy: Post-conceptive Fertility Control*, Sydney, Australia, Angus & Robertson, p. 220.
BG Walker, 1983, *The Women's Encyclopaedia of Myths and Secrets*, New York, Harper & Row, p. 104.

Taking a close look at the assumptions and laws that have determined our life choices is the beginning of being able to choose rather than be controlled by factors that are usually invisible and taken for granted. There is no doubt that cultural beliefs shape our lives[6], and it requires great effort to see beyond what we have been taught to believe. Despite centuries of conditioning, many of us can sense that things are not what they seem, that so-called 'experts' don't always know best. One of the things that supports this sort of intuitive knowing is the relationship women have with our bodies via sexuality, menstruation, pregnancy, childbirth, and hands on parenting.

In my PhD research[7], I spoke with women who practise various forms of reproductive autonomy. These women have found their own ways to manage fertility outside contemporary reproductive beliefs and practices. Some women use imagery and body sensing to prevent implantation of the fertilised egg; some say "No" to the spirit of the child wanting to enter; some visualise a barrier that protects the womb; others describe variations on these processes.

---

[6] T Kuhn, 1962, *The Structure of Scientific Revolutions,* University of Chicago Press, Chicago.
One of the most influential historians of science, Thomas Kuhn has described how objective, impersonal scientific facts can be understood as belief systems which, although true, are not an expression of absolute truth. In other words, just because something can be shown to be true, it does not mean that it is the only truth, or the only way to make sense of our experience. From this perspective, science is just another mythology, and the so-called facts of our own time and place may, indeed, be similar to the 'superstitions" of another time and place. In my studies, I have discovered both facts and superstitions that help to explain the idea and experience of mindbody birth control and birth control more generally.
[7] HK Cargill, 1999, *A Phenomenological Investigation of a Psychobiological Method of Birth Control,* Doctoral thesis held at Monash University, Clayton, Victoria, Australia.

What they all have in common is that they

- are dissatisfied with conventional birth control methods;
- value choice, control and empowerment in fertility management;
- are ruthless in their determination to have no (more) children;
- have actively sought a viable alternative method of birth control;
- assume this is possible outside the existing forms;
- approach the alternative practices of birth control with concentration and commitment;
- experience a permeability between conscious and unconscious processes and experience.

Ruthlessness may be the most difficult of these for contemporary women. Consider this comment on woman's attitude to abortion:

It is man who has evolved principles about the sacredness of life (which he very imperfectly lives up to) and women have passionately adopted them as their own. But principles are abstract ideas which are not, I believe, inherent in feminine psychology. Woman's basic instincts are not concerned with the idea of life as such, but with the fact of life. The ruthlessness of nature which discards unwanted life is deeply ingrained in her make-up.[8]

Culturally, we have become accustomed to educated, intelligent women "taking it like a man"[9], and we interpret ruthlessness as competitiveness or the drive for success and achievement. Yet women's capacity for ruthlessness can have a very different focus. In terms of procreation, we are familiar with the ruthlessness of the mother in protecting her young, yet there is also a ruthlessness in refusing a foetus a place in which to grow, a ruthless determination

---

[8] de Castillejo, op cit., p. 94.

[9] M Woodman, 1985, *The Pregnant Virgin: A Process of Psychological Transformation*, Toronto, Inner City Books, pp. 33-53.

in protecting an egg from fertilisation, a ruthlessness in saying "No" to the spirit of a child who wants to enter the womb.

Refusing to allow the spirit of the child to enter is one approach used by women practicing reproductive autonomy.[10] Robyn, in her late thirties, and a mother of three teenagers, did not want any more children. She described "*the point of saying no to the being who might enter*" in her birth control practice. For Robyn, the biological process was not an important part of controlling conception, even though she had a clear understanding of the reproductive cycle. Instead, she placed emphasis on her spiritual beliefs, describing at length the relevance of her spiritual practice to her experience of regulating conception;

> *The point of saying "No" is to the being who might enter. A prayer of asking that sexual sharing is a process of worship and if it is to do with my will, I do not wish to have a child... and ask to be protected from a child that does not really need to come.*

Amy, a 50-year-old teacher who spoke of "power, spirit, and ancestral worship" in tribal cultures, described her practice as... *a thought perception rather than physical.... very much out there. I'm sure there is something for people to connect with.*

Participant-observation[11] of the Trobriand Islanders in the early 1900s found that the Islanders did not make any connection between sexual intercourse and pregnancy. Pregnancy only occurred when a woman "invited the spirit of a child to enter her body". The Trobrianders had strong taboos against pregnancy in unmarried girls, yet there were no taboos against premarital sex, and young people often lived together, having frequent sexual contact. Pregnancy rarely occurred in such relationships, but there were no obvious forms of contraception, and abstinence was not

---

[10] HK Cargill, op. cit. Interviews with Australian women practising reproductive autonomy.

[11] B Malinowski, 1929, *The Sexual Life of Savages*, New York, Harcourt, Brace, & World.

practised. The Trobrianders simply believed that girls who did not invite the spirit of the child into their bodies would not conceive. The same girls, once married, invited the spirit of the child to enter and had no difficulty conceiving.

There are other cross-cultural examples of mindbody birth control. In the Muria culture of India[12] young people from five to seventeen lived separately from their parents in a "ghotul" dormitory. Within the ghotul, the teenagers had regular sexual relations, but only 4 percent of the young women became pregnant before marriage. Upon entering the ghotul, each girl took part in a ceremony in which the 'God' of the ghotul was requested to keep her from becoming pregnant before marriage. Think about it: this was the only contraceptive measure used, yet they maintained a 96% success rate. The strong belief in the 'God' of the ghotul allowed these girls to practice mindbody birth control.

Another story comes out of Africa. A field researcher with whom I corresponded described a local practice in which a woman would jump one way across a bush in order to conceive and the other way in order not to conceive.[13] This worked well unless the bush disappeared between visits!

It does seem that however we explain what we are doing, women can devise ways to manage fertility that offer true reproductive autonomy. So much depends on the prevailing beliefs of the culture.

Take some time to consider these alternative belief systems. It can seem strange that some groups of people have not recognised the connection between sexual intercourse and pregnancy. This connection seems obvious to us because it has become part of the cultural reality, but our knowledge of sexual reproduction is not innate. We are taught the information very much as the Muria children learned about the 'God' of the ghotul and children in other

---

[12] A Rosenblum, 1976, *The Natural Birth Control Book*, Philadelphia, PA, Aquarian Research Foundation.
[13] Private correspondence, 1993, Dr Vincent Priya, Malawi, Africa.

cultures learn about the belief structures by which their elders make sense of the world. We need only listen to children in primary school wondering whether "kissing will make you pregnant", or whether a girl "gets pregnant through her belly button" to see this. Just over one hundred years ago, nineteenth century medicine was still debating theories of menstruation, with some physicians arguing that it was a pathology. The universal belief, with very few exceptions during the nineteenth century, was that conception occurred at menstruation. This belief persisted into the twentieth century and was only definitely disproved about 90 years ago.[14] The understanding of reproduction that we take for granted is a relatively recent discovery. There are many ways of thinking about conception and contraception. It could be that the idea of a symbolic creativity like that of the Trobriand Islanders is actually a higher order of thinking than our reliance on facts based on observations of the physical body.[15]

The biological role of the male in impregnation was often not given credence in ancient history and mythology. Women impregnated by means not involving mortal men have been described in myths from biblical times to more recent historical eras, and parthenogenesis (conception without male involvement) is also often described, with women becoming pregnant autonomously, without the fertilisation of man or God. In fact, spontaneous generation has been the subject of contemporary research, with somewhat astonishing results. Scientists have reported techniques of activation of eggs (silkworm, mouse, and bovine) toward parthenogenetic development.[16]

---

[14] Davis, op. cit.

[15] G Lerner, 1986, *The Creation of Patriarchy*, New York, Oxford University Press, p. 151.

[16] D Lechniak, D Cieslak, & J Sosnowski, 1998, Morphology and developmental potential of bovine parthenotes after spontaneous activation in vitro, in *Journal of Applied Genetics, 39,* pp. 193-198.
P Loi, S Ledda, J Fulka Jr, P Cappai, & RM Moor, 1998, Development of parthenogenetic and cloned ovine embryos: effect of activation protocols, in *Biology of Reproduction, 58,* pp. 1177-1187.

Ignorance about the causal relationship between sexual intercourse and pregnancy was also observed among traditional groups in New Guinea, and among the Arunta in Central Australia.[17] One contemporary researcher found that to the Aboriginal mind, the modern explanation of conception as the collision of sperm and egg is absurd. In their view, sperm may prepare the way for the entry of the child into the womb, but the spirit of the child appears in the father's dreams or inner awareness before conception.[18]

S Nimura & T Asami, 1997, A histochemical study of the steroid metabolism in parthenogenetic mouse blastocysts, in *Journal of Reproduction and Development, 43*, pp. 251-256.

R Singh, MM Ahsan, & RK Datta, 1997, Artificial parthenogenesis in the silkworm Bombyx mori L., in *Indian Journal of Sericulture, 36*, pp. 87-91.

[17] B Spencer & FJ Gillen, 1904, *The Northern Tribes of Central Australia*, London, Macmillan & Co.

Spencer & Gillen began studying the Arunta people of Central Australia in 1896, before exposure to European settlers. Their report of initiation rites among the Arunta is hundreds of pages long and has been used as a reference for ancient practices which have seldom been observed in a relatively isolated culture. Malinowski, 1974, op. cit., p. 232.

[18] R Lawlor, 1991, *Voices of the First day: Awakening the Aboriginal Dreamtime*, Vermont, VT: Inner Traditions International, Ltd., p.159.

There are stories of spontaneous abortion which suggest that many of the practices observed in pre-industrial cultures are about controlling rather than increasing fertility (see M Harris & E Ross, 1987, *Death, Sex, and Fertility*, New York, Columbia University Press.) This may have been especially prevalent among prehistoric foragers, where being able to control fertility in response to climate, food supply, mobility of the group, and other conditions may have ensured survival. Consistent with this, it was found that Aboriginal men do not consider children a means of perpetuating their individual achievements. Their understanding is that continued fertility has only become important in cultures where the emphasis is on owning land and overcoming nature to set up powerful agricultural settlements (Lawlor, p. 163). Observations of Aboriginal childbearing and rearing practices indicated that the low, stable Aboriginal population was due to the innate ability of the women to regulate conception and childbirth and avoid unnecessary birth, and that it is the patriarchal social order which has eroded this ability.

It seems that indigenous Australians also believed, and experienced, that a woman can be spiritually fertilised by coming into contact with a power related to a specific place:

> Every ancestor, while chanting his or her way across the land during the Dreamtime, also deposited a trail of "spirit children" along the line of his footsteps. These "life cells" are children not yet born: they lie in a kind of potential state in the ground, waiting. While sexual intercourse between a man and a woman is thought, by traditional Aboriginal persons, to prepare the woman for conception, the actual conception is assumed to occur much later, when the already pregnant woman is out on her daily rounds gathering roots and edible grubs, and she happens to step upon (or even near) a song couplet. The "spirit child" lying beneath the ground at that spot slips up into her at that moment.[19]

This magical story of conception takes baby making out of the purely physical, inviting us to think beyond what we have taken for granted. Regardless of which story we believe, women across cultures have been using their own methods to manage fertility. A strongly held belief or experience of the natural and supernatural worlds made conception impossible under certain conditions –
people in many pre-industrial cultures simply did not believe that pregnancy could occur under certain conditions and, in the majority of cases, it did not. These stories are important because they invite us to think beyond what we know as 'truth', challenging our conditioned beliefs and suggesting new possibilities. Imagine what can happen when we loosen the bindings of our conditioned perception.

---

[19] D Abram, 1996, *The spell of the Sensuous: Perception and Language in a More-Than-Human World*, New York, Vintage Books, p. 167.

Anthropologist, Margaret Mead[20], said this:

> Behind all of these age-old devices (contraception, abortion, infanticide) there lies a subtler factor, a willingness or an unwillingness to breed that is deeply imbedded in the character structure of both men and women. How these relative willingnesses and unwillingnesses function, at what point in the reproductive process blocks are introduced, we still do not know, but the evidence leaves little doubt that they are there…

> … It is possible that we may someday evolve a culture in which there will be such a good communication within each paired relationship that no other control will be needed than the female's own natural monthly rhythm of fertility.[21]

There is, therefore, a bigger story behind the current issues with abortion. I wish all women could step away from needing permission from law makers, but thousands of years of patriarchal conditioning and persecution make that impossible. Nevertheless I think we need to be fighting this at all levels – the obvious level of demanding legal rights to abortion on demand, and the less obvious level of remembering how we got to this point and how we can reclaim true reproductive autonomy.

---

[20] M Mead, 1959, *Male and Female: A Study of the Sexes in a Changing World*, New York, Mentor Books, pp. 171-2.
[21] ibid. pp. 181-2.

An invitation:

Imagine that you have grown up in a culture like the Trobriand Islands, or an imaginary place where the belief system supports sexual freedom and your right to manage fertility through some sort of ritual or internal mindbody process.

What would your fertility management process be? Would it involve a God or Goddess or some other deity? Would it involve the rhythms and cycles of your body? Something else?

Write this as a story, an alternate herstory. Allow your imagination to inform you how mindbody birth control can work for you. What are the elements of this? It may be a daily practice, or something that you only do on the full moon, or when your menstruation is due. It may be something elaborate or something simple. Take some time to find your relationship with the deep feminine mysteries that support this way of experiencing yourself.

If this calls to you, you may want to read more about mindbody birth control and reproductive autonomy – *Don't Take It Lying Down: Life According to the Goddess.*

Aoife's Healing

Dee Mulrooney

False Spring

Raven Bishop

I wrote this poem days after attending the 2017 Women's March in Washington, D.C. The days before the march had been unseasonably warm and many trees had begun to flower. Then a cold front had come through—the flowering trees took a frost and the delicate petals had turned brown. Walking under those trees, listening to the rustling of those battered blossoms holding on in the wind seemed prescient and inspired this poem which I have returned to many times in prayer and ceremony throughout the past several years.

False Spring

There is a storm coming
in this false Spring
whose spectre
hangs heavy upon just-bloomed
cherry blossoms
which rustle in the wind
like brittle browned pages of antique grimoires

Walking beneath these boughs
I am thinking of grannies
who witnessed their sisters
hung from these self-same trees
or drowned ducking
in the floodwaters of fear

Sisters, you took their books
hid them beneath floorboards
and between walls
hiding their knowledge
in star-wishes and birthday cakes

while you served their daughters
pennyroyal tea
taught them to honey their thighs
And be more careful next time

There is a storm coming
in this false Spring
pink yarn adorns the crowns
of the granddaughters
and the crones
who march beneath these cherry blossoms

Grannies, you have taught us well
as tomes rot under floorboards
and between walls
their knowledge is written in our skin
and courses through
blood and honey

We shall keep
proud sparks in fire pots
as snow falls upon cherry blossoms
in this false Spring

Into the Silence

Raven Bishop

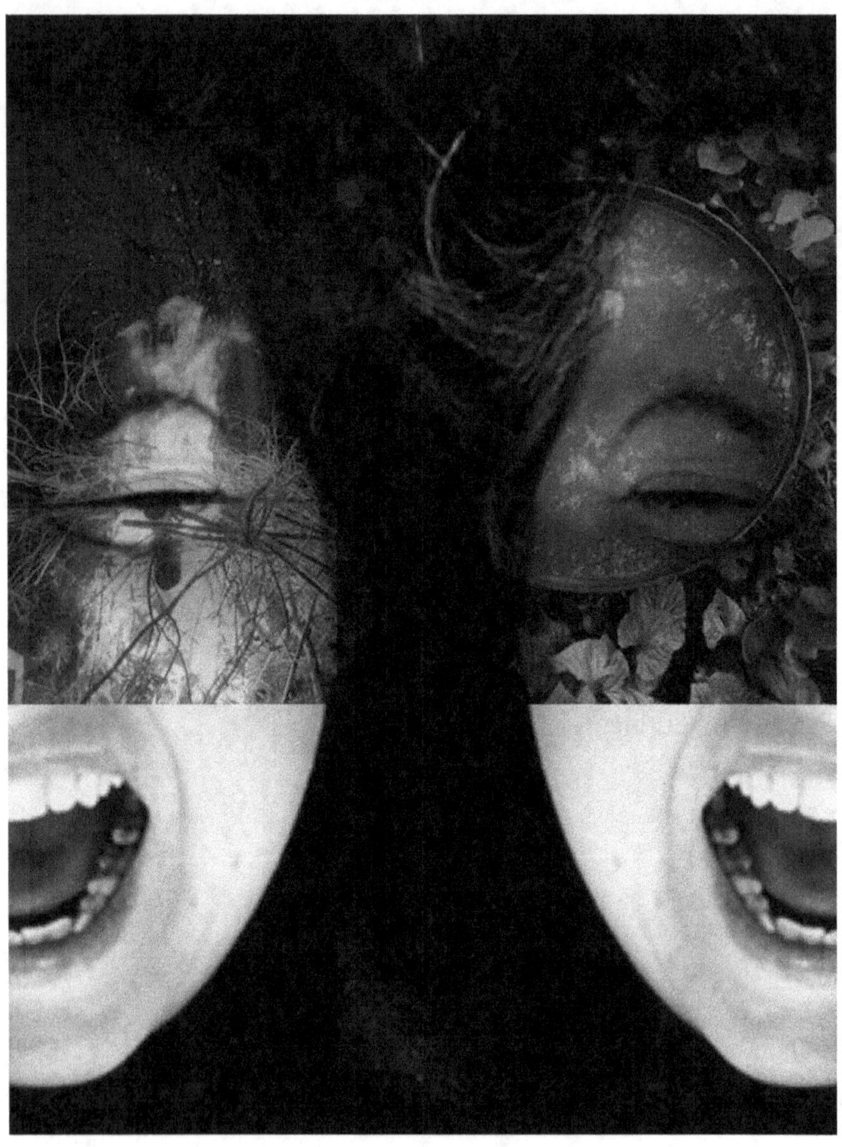

As I have been processing first the spectre, then the threat, then the actual overturning of Roe v. Wade, I have felt a silent scream rising up in my soul. I am not a woman who knows how to keep silent—but this particular scream seemed blocked and has yet to audibly emerge. I created this work to release this scream, overlaying a self-portrait of my silent scream on images captured in my practice of elemental ceremony and prayer—the place I have turned to in moments when my scream would not or could not escape.

Our Lady Colossus

Raven Bishop

I wrote this poem after the Kavanaugh Supreme Court confirmation in an attempt to transform my rage into something—productive?—useful?—into something else—into some *thing*. My heart was seeking a powerful goddess to embody women's collective rage. An image of the Statue of Liberty stepping down off her plinth, striding across our nation, a throng of women fighting for justice marching in her wake battle came to my mind, leading me to revisit Emma Lazarus' famous work, "The New Colossus". Reinterpreting her work gave me a way of deifying this iconic female symbol of our nation and giving shape to this vision of her as a goddess for these times.

Our Lady Colossus

Not like the brazen giants of greed and fame,
With conquering machinations astride from land to land;
Here at our tear-washed, sweat-stained gates does stand
A mighty woman with a torch, whose flame
Is the imprisoned lightning of women's rage.
Mother of Mothers.

From her beacon-hand
Glows world-wide rancor; her embattled eyes command
The divided nation that twin aisles frame
As she descends from her plinth, begins to quake.
And in her patinaed, carved-sandaled stride,
She calls her daughters to her side,
To join the march from shore to shore,
Hell hath no fury...

In the days when justice wears robes of shame,
Our Lady Colossus wields her flame.
"Keep, ancient men, your storied pomp!" cries she
With lips no longer silent.
Commands her sons,
"Keep your tired, your poor,
Your flagrant lies, yearning to condemn,
The wretched refuse of your wanton waning power.
See these, the fearless, tempest-tost sisters with me,
By my lamp, we will be your end!"

My Body, My Choice
Barbara O'Meara

Raising My Voice!

Karen Storminger

On June 24, 2022, the Supreme Court of the United States of America overturned the 1973 court ruling on Roe v. Wade and began the descent of American women back into the dark ages of reproductive health care. I will never forget that day, nor the names of the justices who supported the decision to overturn based upon their own personal beliefs and not upon the objectiveness of modern law. It is one huge blow to the rights and liberties of female citizens of this country and an obvious attempt to control and maintain power over half the population.

When I heard the news that day I cried, I screamed, I raged, I cursed, and I vowed to act.

The signs leading up to this reversal were evident: pharmacists refusing to fill contraceptive prescriptions, corporations deciding they don't believe they should have to cover contraceptives under their insurance for their workers, and the removal of funding for Planned Parenthood. Since this reversal decision, in states across the country we have seen the passing of trigger laws and bans, which excessively restrict the access to abortion, and seek to make it impossible for women to receive necessary medical care, abortion information and alternatives.

This impacts every woman; however, it seriously and severely impacts minority women, the poor and the underprivileged. The poor rely on women's healthcare clinics like Planned Parenthood for more than just abortions – they can receive important medical care outside of reproduction! This is personal to me as a woman, as a citizen, as an educator and as someone who has had to make these same tough decisions in her life. Even though I live in a state which supports a woman's right to choose, I fear for my daughter who is at risk of losing her right to decide what is best for her life. I fear for her very life itself if I am to be truthful.

These issues have all been swirling around in my head. I sorely wanted to say something to someone about how frustratingly wrong this all is, how damaging to the direction of women's rights this is all going. It has taken women in this country over one hundred years to achieve some semblance of physical and intellectual autonomy. To have the right to vote, to work outside the home, to get an education of our own choosing, to live and love whomever we want and by our own leave. To work in jobs once thought of as only a man's domain and to excel at them. Women have fought for these rights, quite literally at times. Those who came before us faced jail, beatings, ostracism, and death for speaking their minds. How dare we let them down now by allowing things to disintegrate before our eyes! We have only just dipped a toe in the water of equality and equity. Now there are those who would drag us back into subservience and inequality. My anger grows with every news report. What does one do when faced with unacceptable rhetoric, bigotry, misogyny, and an attack on their very right to liberty and pursuit of happiness in this country? She Raises Her Voice. This is my story.

I was twenty-one, I was a sophomore in community college, working part-time and dating a guy I loved, but who had issues of his own. During this time, I found out I was pregnant. I was afraid I'd have to quit school. I knew getting married would be difficult, even though I loved him, and I wasn't sure I could manage being a mother at the time. I went to the local Planned Parenthood. I received excellent medical care, tests which confirmed that yes, I was indeed pregnant, and counseling which gave me all the facts about having a healthy pregnancy and all the options available to me to make an informed decision as to what I wanted to do. I had sonograms taken to determine how far along I was in my pregnancy and all options for keeping or aborting were explained to me. I went back and forth to that clinic multiple times for appointments and spoke to more than one doctor. I did not take my decision lightly. No one I know in this type of situation is blasé about such a life altering decision. Anyone who tells you women use abortions as a form of birth control is out of touch with reality. There are cheaper and far less physically and emotionally rending forms of birth control available. In the end, I made the decision for myself to keep my pregnancy and have my baby. It was my decision, not the father's. Even he agreed that it was my decision to make, as it was my body, and it was my life that would change dramatically either way. I kept my pregnancy. I gave birth to a beautiful son who I cherish and believe I was meant to mother. It was my decision, and I do not regret making it.

Nine months later, I was excitedly preparing to re-enter college and complete my bachelor's degree in education. I had a good part-time job working with a friend who would also be caring for my son while I was in class. I was married and we were struggling with our little family, we had issues, but we were trying to make things work. My birth control failed, I skipped my period and panicked. I went immediately to the doctor again and confirmed I was pregnant, again. Once more I asked questions and took all the information I was given and went home to think and make a difficult decision for myself. I was struggling already to pay bills, put food on the table and in a relationship that was at times volatile. Having a second child at that time would have put us on government assistance, pushed back my re-entry to college or even ended my ability to complete my degree – which would have put us into perpetual financial difficulty. I decided to have an abortion. I did not make that decision lightly or easily. I still stand by that decision with no regrets because it was what was best for me, my life, and future and for the child I already had.

The years passed and my marriage had its difficulties. I finished college, received my bachelor's degree, received my teaching certification, got a good teaching job and we eventually bought a home and seemed to be doing well, living the "dream." We decided to have a second child then and were happy to become the parents of an amazing baby girl. We had a boy and a girl, a home, and careers we had worked extremely hard for over the years. We still had problems, but that is life. A year after my daughter was born, we found out I was pregnant with baby number three. We hadn't been trying to get pregnant, but we hadn't been not trying either.

Everything seemed fine and once we got through the first trimester; we announced the expansion of our family to our relatives and friends. It wouldn't be easy, but we'd make it work, I thought. Eighteen weeks into my pregnancy at my regular checkup there was silence in the exam room as my OB had difficulty finding a heartbeat. He did a sonogram in the office. The looks and silence of both the nurse and him said it all. There was something very wrong with my pregnancy. I went home crying and told my husband.

The next day I made an appointment at the hospital for a higher-level sonogram to be done to see what exactly was happening. I had to wait two more weeks to be seen. Two agonizing weeks of anxiety waiting for answers. When the test was finally done, I was given the devastating news that the baby was not fully formed in utero. Limb-body-stalk anomaly is what I was told. The fetus still had a heartbeat and should have naturally miscarried given the extent of the defects that were visible to the doctors. I should have miscarried, but I hadn't and carrying the pregnancy to term was dangerous. I was told my baby would die in utero. If that happened, I would be at risk for sepsis and I could die as well. If the baby lived to term, survived the labor and delivery, it would most definitely die within a brief time after birth in excruciating pain. These were my choices. I could have a medically necessary abortion and go home to live and raise my two children. I could risk dying and leaving my children without their mother. Or I could watch this baby die in front of me in unnecessary pain and suffering while also risking my life in that scenario as well. This was a choice I would never wish upon my worst enemy. However, it was still MY CHOICE. Not my husband's, not my insurance carrier, not my doctor's, not my legislator's, not my neighbor's, my government's, or anyone else's. My choice, for my body and my life. I chose to have the abortion. It tore me up inside emotionally and took me years to heal from both physically and mentally.

However, I am here today. I have two grown, amazing, and independent adult children making their own way in this world. I have a fulfilling professional career, a home, a new relationship, and a great life. I do not regret any of my decisions because they were informed, educated, and well thought out. Most important they were mine to make: I determined the path of my own life. If those decisions had been taken from me by laws and bans which restricted my access to care and information at that time, the outcome for me and my family would have been drastically different. I would not have been a teacher or had the chance to work with the most amazing students over the years. I would not have been in a position financially, without my education, to get out of a dysfunctional marriage and take care of myself and my children. I may not even be here today, alive.

Right now, the average American has the right to drink, smoke, and make other medical decisions unencumbered. This is true even if that decision is to refuse vaccinations based on their personal beliefs, thereby putting at risk the lives of anyone in contact with them if they were to contract a preventable contagious disease. It is also true, that depending upon which state they live in today, the average American woman does not have the right to make a life altering, quite possibly a life-or-death medical decision, to end her own pregnancy. These disparities have nothing to do with the sanctity of life and are not Pro-Life. Saving lives is not what reversing Roe v. Wade has ever been about. If that were the case, then birth control and preventative health care would be free, readily, and equally available for all citizens. Children would not languish in foster care and the United States would not have one of the highest maternal mortality rates of any developed nation, even before the reversal (CDC.gov). The reversal of Roe v. Wade is in fact predicted to increase the likelihood of infant and maternal mortality due to a person's inability to access needed medical care in the states already putting strict bans in place. It is predicted that the maternal homicide rate will increase as well. (Abortion Bans and Maternal Mortality Rate, Andrea Rice, Healthline.com July 27, 2022.)

This is my story. It happened to me and may resonate with other women out there right now. It is important because the ability to make those informed and educated, personal liberty choices are systematically being taken away from thousands of women every day in states across this country. I am angered that someone else may face a different outcome, may lose her life, because her legislators pander to the groups with money, allowing zealots to impose their own judgement upon these decisions, taking them away from the individual. We have the fundamental right to life, liberty, and the pursuit of happiness in this country. This phrase and these "unalienable rights" are part of the Declaration of Independence, the beginning basis of our country that states that these rights are to be protected by government, not denied. How dare any human take away that right from one half of the population!

I am telling my story, supporting local abortion funds groups, and using my right to protest. These are my current actions since this reversal. I'm raising my voice; I encourage others to do so as well. Together, our voices united can make a world of difference. RAISE YOUR VOICE!

References

Maternal Mortality is Likely to Rise Post-Roe: The Reasons May Surprise You (Healthline.com)

Homicide is a top cause of maternal death in the United States (nature.com)

Maternal Mortality Rates in the United States:
www.cdc.gov/nchs/data/hestat/maternal-mortality/2020/maternal-mortality-rates-2020.htm

I Own the Skin I'm In

Kat Shaw

the cathedral, a big building, a thing of the past, obsolete, to excite him to such a pitch? She began to stir herself to readiness.

They passed up the steep hill, he eager as a pilgrim arriving at the shrine. As they came near the precincts, with castle on one side and cathedral on the other his veins seemed to break into fiery blossom, he was transported.

They had passed through the gate, and the great west front was before them, with all its breadth and ornament.

'It is a false front,' he said, looking at the golden stone and the twin towers, and loving them just the same. In a little ecstasy he found himself in the porch, on the brink of the unrevealed. He looked up to the lovely unfolding of the stone. He was to pass within to the perfect womb.

Then he pushed open the door, and the great, pillared gloom was before him, in which his soul shuddered and rose from her nest. His soul leapt, soared up into the great church. His body stood still, absorbed by the height. His soul leapt up into the gloom, into possession, it reeled, it swooned with a great escape, it quivered in the womb, in the hush and the gloom of fecundity, like seed of procreation in ecstasy.

She too was overcome with wonder and awe. She followed him in his progress. Here the twilight was the very essence of life, the coloured darkness was the embryo of all light, and the day. Here the very first dawn was breaking, the very last sunset sinking, and the immemorial darkness, whereof life's day would blossom and fall away again, re-echoed peace and profound immemorial silence.

Away from time, always outside of time! Between east and west, between dawn and sunset, the church lay like a seed in silence, dark before germination, silenced after death. Containing birth and death, potential with all the noise and transition of life, the cathedral remained hushed, a great, involved seed, whereof the flower would be radiant life inconceivable, but whose beginning and whose end were the circle of silence. Spanned round with the rainbow, the jewelled gloom folded music upon silence, light upon darkness, fecundity upon death as a seed folds leaf upon leaf and silence upon the root and the

"Fuck you!"

Karen Storminger

He said,
"God is punishing me, that is why this is happening to you."
No.
To you and your selfish pity.
I say, "Fuck you!"
Your "Father" God,
who spreads his seed about without want to care where,
when, or what will happen to it once it sprouts.
No.
To your patriarchal God,
I say, "Fuck you!"
My fate is my own.
My choices are mine.
I faced a life-or-death situation.
I faced a choice no woman should have to make.
But I did.
I chose to mother my babes asleep in their beds.
You wallowed in fake tears of self-pity.
You spoke of a God who punishes you by hurting others.
In this God you trust?!
Fuck you! I do not!
Your God is not a Great Creator.
A God of men who brings only destruction, revenge,
fear and intolerance, power over others.
Fuck you!
I am closer to the true Divine than you or him.
My body is a portal,
through which the natural cycles of life and death,
become a part of the world.
The two connected by a thread.
Dancing upon opposite sides of the precipice.
I stand upon that precipice.

Bearing down, I have brought forth life, joy, beauty,
from this portal.
I have faced Death.
I have handed Death a piece of me to watch over until we meet
again.
Fuck your God of Hate and subjugation!
My Goddess is life and death intertwined.
Free will and self-determination.
Joy, peace, battle, grief.
The sweet taste of dawn the morning after.
While you whined and sat useless, blaming another,
I stood and faced the challenge.
I made my choice.
I fought to live.
He said,
"God is punishing me...."
I said,
"Fuck you both!"

Sheelas

Liz Darling

A Modest Proposal

Bambi Lobdell, PhD

On January 22, 1973, the Supreme Court ruled that the Due Process Clause of the 14th Amendment implied a right to privacy, and therefore, abortion was protected as a fundamental right. On June 24, 2022, The Supreme Court overturned abortion rights, arguing abortion was not guaranteed by the Constitution, and left abortion access up to the states. In September of 2022, Senate Republicans, led by Lindsey Graham of South Carolina, introduced a federal bill to make abortions illegal after fifteen weeks, with exceptions for rape, incest, and risk of the mother's life (Durkee).

Many people thought that the right to abortion (with certain limitations) was settled law. Abortion, considered a very private matter, is not a topic of general discussion. People thought if someone needed an abortion, they could get one. And complacency set it.

However, conservatives have been working toward overturning Roe since abortion was legalized in 1973. Driven by moral righteousness, the main Conservative argument against abortion is that life is sacred, begins at conception, and needs to be protected. Members of the Ethics and Religious Liberty Commission of the Southern Baptist Convention claim to be working to protect "the dignity of human life" by making abortion illegal. Even though they recognize "there will still be thousands of women who will face an unplanned pregnancy [and] many of them will be afraid, unprepared, and unsure of what to do and where to turn", they still want to ban all abortions. Ignoring issues of economic status, age, safety, and life goals, this group proposes to "reach abortion-minded and abortion-vulnerable women where they are and speak with compassion, empathy, and relevancy to their situations, which are often messy, complex, band dire." Yet, no solutions for poverty or domestic abuse or interrupted goals for career, school, or needs of already existing families – often determining factors in considering abortion – are discussed at all (The Ethics and Religious Liberty Commission of the Southern Baptist Convention).

Human Life International presents manipulated statistics about the percentages of abortions performed to save the life of the mother, deal with birth defects, or resolve a pregnancy from rape or incest, claiming each category makes up around 1% or less of abortions performed, which greatly dilutes the most acceptable reasons for abortion. They manipulate statistics from the well-respected Guttmacher Institute in a way that eliminates specific reasons by stating "96.50% of all abortions are therefore performed for social or economic reasons". Without discussing any details concerning those social or economic reasons, they claim that these women have abortions "to preserve the mother's lifestyle or please those near her", which seems to imply these women replaced responsibility and morality with selfishness and have no reverence for life (Human Life International). These organizations offer no discussion of poverty or lack of resources to raise a child, child care or health care, or cost of housing or food, and no discussion of domestic violence.

The Guttmacher Institute gives more detailed reasons people get abortions, and a much more nuanced discussion. Their statistics reveal that "the two most common reasons [for getting an abortion] were "having a baby would dramatically change my life" and "I can't afford a baby now" (cited by 74% and 73%, respectively). A further breakdown reveals that having a baby would interfere with education or employment/career goals. 73% of people who got abortions stated they could not afford a baby now because they were unmarried, or a student, or could not afford childcare or basic needs like housing and food, were unemployed, or did not receive enough support from the father. 48% of women cited relationship problems as the reason for abortion (Guttmacher Institute).

These statistics spotlight that having a baby is often a financial hardship for the person who raises it. As a society, we expect the new mother to be the one to take the baby home from the hospital, to lovingly raise that child, provide shelter, food, clothes, health care, attention, and make sure it gets an education. To do so for at least eighteen years requires time and sacrifice of other goals, like education and career. And it costs a lot of money, which is why so many women with children end up living in or near poverty. Debates about abortion rarely include these issues.

Some people have argued that men need to step up and be responsible for life they help to create. On the surface, this would make a lot of sense and seem to solve economic aspects of this issue. The problem is that after the development of DNA testing, that approach was tried, through legislation requiring men to pay child support. The result? Homicide became, and remains, the leading cause of death in pregnant women in the United States: "Homicide during pregnancy or within 42 days of the end of pregnancy exceeded all the leading causes of maternal mortality by more than twofold" (Wallace, et al).

Considering the reality for pregnant people and the various reasons for seeking abortion, the argument that the fetus should be protected because life is sacred falls flat. People seek abortions because of economic insecurity and the threat of violence. Yet these problems are not addressed well in our society. The Pro-Life movement is largely comprised of conservatives and Republicans, and yet those same people tend to undermine legislation that would give assistance and resources to mothers, like pre-natal health care, childcare, food, housing, Pre-K, and healthcare.

Even some Republican lawmakers are taking issue and pointing out the misogyny and hypocrisy. South Carolina Republican Senator Katrina Shealy – a woman with pro-life beliefs – rejected proposals to repeal abortion rights. She angrily pointed out that the men in the chamber were not OBGYNs, and had no experience with menstrual cycles, conception, or pregnancy. She does not believe that life and death decisions should be made by legislators who want to restrict doctors from doing what is best for their patients. Shealy accused the men of being more concerned with claiming a political victory than truly caring about mothers and babies, or the potential for them to be living in poverty and experiencing domestic abuse.

> You will fight my legislation for foster homes and adoption. You will not support legislation to stop sex trafficking and pornography. You will not support my legislation for free meals for all children in schools. You're not going to help me on that.

Shealy's speech makes clear the hypocrisy of those who claim to want to protect children. She then makes that sad appeal to the men to think about their wives and daughters, granddaughters and nieces, in an attempt to humanize women, instead of treating them only as commodities to manage and use to reinforce their own status and power (Katrina Shealy Responds).

The hypocrisy of many of those in the Pro-Life movement was pointed out years ago. In a 2004 interview with Bill Moyers, Sister Joan Chittister says:

> I do not believe that just because you're opposed to abortion, that that makes you pro-life. In fact, I think in many cases, your morality is deeply lacking if all you want is a child born but not a child fed, not a child educated, not a child housed. And why would I think that you don't? Because you don't want any tax money to go there. That's not pro-life. That's pro-birth. We need a much broader conversation on what the morality of pro-life is. (Chittister on the Meaning of Life).

At least in Gilead they took care of the babies....

If our society truly valued mothers and the work they do in raising children, it would do more than send sweet cards and flowers on Mother's Day. It would support people who *do* want children, and alleviate the problems brought on by poverty and lack of health care. A group of Black female legislators is working toward that very goal. On February 8, 2021, Representative Lauren Underwood introduced H. R. 959 – the Black Maternal Health Momnibus:

> This bill directs multi-agency efforts to improve maternal health, particularly among racial and ethnic minority groups, veterans, and other vulnerable populations. The Department of Health and Human Services (HHS) and other specified departments must address the social determinants of maternal health, which include child care, housing, food security, transportation, and environmental conditions. The bill also extends to 24 months postpartum eligibility for the Special Supplemental Nutrition Program for Woman, Infants, and Children. Additionally, HHS and other agencies must take actions to grow and diversify the maternal health workforce. (H. R. 959)

Conservative actions restricting access to abortion in an effort to protect the unborn fall apart when it comes to their support of Herschel Walker. Walker claims to be a staunch Pro-Life candidate in his race for the Georgia Senate in 2022, and revels in the praise and prayers he receives from his supporters. But his son, Christian Walker, himself a Conservative, blasted his father for having a number of children out of wedlock and being absent in raising any of them (Walker Goes Off). Additionally, *The New York Times* reported that Walker paid for an abortion for one of his girlfriends in 2009, and urged her to have a second abortion in 2012. When she refused, their relationship ended (King, Lerer, Bromwich). And still Republicans embrace Walker in his Senate race against the Reverend Raphael Warnock, the incumbent, who is also the pastor of the Ebenezer Baptist Church – the same church Dr. Martin Luther King Jr, preached in.....

Many Republicans have made it clear they don't really care about the children they want to force to be born. They refuse to pass bills that would provide daycare, housing, food, universal pre-K, WIC, or additional child tax credit. So, what is it they actually want to achieve?? There is a parallel between the Herschel Walker story and the actions of the government: both want access to, possession of, and control over female bodies when it comes to sex and maternity, without the responsibility they owe to the lives they help create. The government acts like an absentee father. And the support for Walker reveals that Republicans don't really care about abortion except to use it as a tool to control and restrict women. It appears to be acceptable when men want to simplify their lives by asking their women to have abortions.

It has not always been this way. The fight for control over female bodies, especially when it comes to bringing forth babies, is not a new one. It is thousands of years old.

Early societies formed around "an economic and political structure called matricentry, or life centered around mothers" (French, 23). Societies followed matrilineal patterns, where inheritance and lineage were passed down from mother to daughter. Women regulated possession of titles, political positions, positions of authority; they held command over use of land and resources and food distribution. Women owned the labor of their children and controlled how that labor was used.

In pre-patriarchal societies, the rules of inheritance maintained a stable society. Instead of fighting over who had control of titles, governing positions, people's labor, or command of land use, those things were peacefully passed from Mother to Daughter. It is simple to know who our mothers are – we can observe a baby being born from a specific body. Jacquetta Hawkes, James Frazer, Margaret Meade and other anthropologists, claim that in the early stages of human development, conception was not understood, so men were not acknowledged as necessary to the creation of new people, and women were thought to be able to bring forth new life by themselves (Stone, 11). In an era before sexual restrictions on women, such lineage is the only one that is clear. There were no social rules on who women could sleep with or how many partners they could have. Paternity was not a concept because it was not integral to the structure or stability of society. People who could get pregnant often did, and babies were born.

Once the role of men was understood in conception, it was used to switch control over inheritance from mother to daughter to father to son. According to Marilyn French, men rose up in rebellion to women 10,000 – 12,000 years ago:

> Women were central to society and they supported men… but [men] wanted children to be theirs instead of women's. To accomplish this transfer, they had to push aside mother-right (the right to name the child and control its labor) and so they invented patrilineality, naming the children for their fathers. But this connection is tricky since fatherhood, before DNA testing, could never be assured. To guarantee paternity they had to control women. Keep them under surveillance, and, in effect, own them." (French, 19)

Because wealth and power came to whoever controlled labor, men's "desire to own children (and therefore their labor) is the root of male dominance, the first aggressive act in the drive towards patriarchy" (French, 53).

Ancient sexual customs in pagan religions celebrated sexuality and women who served the temple did so by having sex with men who visited. Their titles in various societies translate into "holy women", sanctified women", or "the undefiled". Because of their relations with numerous men,

> The children born to these women would be of questionable paternity. Sumerian and Babylonian documents reveal that these women, through their affiliations with the temple complex, owned land and other properties and engaged in extensive business activities. Various accounts report that they were often of wealthy families, well accepted in society. Following the original kinship customs of Goddess religion, children born to

Quadishtu would probably inherit the names, titles and property of their mothers; matrilineal descent would have continued to exist as the inherent social structure of the community. (Stone, 157)

The shift to patrilineal societies and male dominance over women happened centuries before the development of writing, but traces of this struggle are evident in the earliest writings. In that shift, women lost their rights to land and children but were still expected to care for both:

Matricentry, small simple societies centered around mothers, was supplanted by a different moral, economic, and sociopolitical structure. Male-dominant patrilineality... gradually destroyed anarchic egalitarianism and women's high status... Everywhere, even in patrilinies in which fathers "own" children, mothers are still expected to raise and feed the family (French, 51)

Because women continued to willingly take care of children, men came to think that this work was an innate function of being female, a view still held today.

A first sign of men trying to establish patriarchy by restricting and managing female bodies appears in the laws of Uruk in Sumer, about 5,000 years ago: "A new crime appeared, adultery, which only women could commit. Infanticide, the prerogative of fathers, was legal, but abortion performed by women was treason... The second structure to spread and strengthen patriarchy was religion" (Stone, 20). The absence of laws concerning the adultery men might commit make clear that the legal focus was on controlling women's sexuality – not men's – for the purpose of establishing legitimate lineage through male lines.

Reality is formed through the dominant stories told, so this new vision of a male dominant society required new narratives that positioned men as superior to women and deserving of power and authority. To achieve patriarchal structure, existing stories had to be altered and crafted to destroy female autonomy and power. The meanings of symbols and known characters had to be refashioned to support a new world order. Sexual morality for women was invented so men would know who their children were; laws were made and enforced, often with violence. About 3,500 years ago, a new story arose, establishing a male-only creator and introducing man's "God-given right" to control women and their sexuality so they would know who their children were. Perhaps the most influential story in Judeo-Christian culture, Genesis accomplished both.

Most creation stories in pagan and indigenous cultures feature a female deity, known as the Great Goddess, bringing forth the world and all life by herself. The power of the being who created the world was reflected in the gendered social order, so the identity of the Creator God was key to control of society. The first chapter of Genesis undoes earlier understanding of Divine Female Power by presenting a male deity who creates everything. While Genesis One presents God creating men and women at the same time, from the same dust, it is Genesis Two that forms the foundation of patriarchal power. Here, God makes Adam first, then the animals, and last, feeling Adam needed an appropriate companion, He took a rib from Adam to make Eve. Through the unnatural rib-birth, Eve and all generations formed after her owed their very existence to man.

In Genesis Three, the serpent tempts Eve to eat the forbidden fruit of the Tree of Knowledge. She then hands the fruit to Adam who eats it without question. God then doles out punishments. The serpent is condemned to crawl on the ground and lose favor with women. Adam is told he will have to till the ground and grow his own food. God tells Eve, "I will greatly multiply thy sorrow and thy conception; in sorrow thou shall bring forth children; and thy desire shall be to thy husband, and he shall rule over thee" (Genesis 3: 18). In other words, despite being commanded in Genesis Two to go forth, be fruitful, and multiply, God now tells Eve that childbirth is going to hurt. She is restricted to sex only with her husband, who will rule over her. Female subordination is secured as a direct commandment from God.

The details of the story may seem minor, but in pre-patriarchal Goddess worshipping societies, the serpent was a symbol of female knowledge, especially the knowledge to heal. The fruit Eve ate was a fig, the fruit of the tree of life under which the Goddess sat. It became known as an apple when the story moved to Europe where figs do not grow. The symbols of the Goddess's power are recast as symbols of sin. The act of disobedience in the pursuit of knowledge gets interpreted as a lack of restraint of appetite, which always translated to sexual appetite in early Christian thought. Eve's name literally means Mother of All Living – the Great Goddess. In this way, the Great Goddess is demoted, drained of power. The female pursuit of knowledge and the power it brings is vilified and made dangerous. The sharing of the fruit with Adam is interpreted as sexual seduction from a temptress who is bent on leading men away from God. Childbirth is now a painful punishment rather than an act revered for its ability to bring forth new life. And while tilling the ground may seem like hard punishment for Adam, this task now moves the power to decide how land was used and foods were distributed to men instead of women.

The new story about female sexuality was enforced, often brutally, by new laws. Sexual purity becomes a paramount requirement in the *Old Testament*, and women were cloistered and expected to be virgins on their wedding day. If there was no blood on the marriage sheets, the bride was assumed to be defiled and taken into the street and stoned to death. (Deuteronomy 22: 13 – 21).

Perhaps the best-known story of whoredom in the Bible centers on the Phoenician princess, Jezebel, who married Ahab, King of Israel, a city at the center of a fight against paganism. Jezebel brought her pagan religious beliefs, practices, and priests with her, along with the economic connections of trade with a rich but pagan kingdom. After Ahab died, she held the power of the throne until her son came of age, a position considered untenable by powerful men in Israel. A challenge ensued to see whose priests had the most powerful deity, and Jezebel lost. She was thrown from her tower and fed to wild dogs. While her religion was the reason the Israelites hated and destroyed her, they conveniently linked the threat of paganism to the new sexual morality for women they were trying to enforce. The spelling of her name before the Bible was written translated to Virgin of Ba'al. One letter was added by the Levite priests and the new spelling translated into Whore of Ba'al (Naked Archeologist). Remember, whoever controls crafting and circulating the story controls reality. To this day, the name "Jezebel" is synonymous with "promiscuous woman".

Narratives were an effective tool in reinforcing male dominance over women. In the 5th century A.D., Augustine wrote *The City of God*, an enormously influential book read even today. In it, he reinforces ideas about women formed from interpretations of Eve, and all of womankind emerges in the three-fold role of temptress, wife, or mother. Augustine argues that without male control, woman can only be a temptress, a tool of the Devil, bent on destroying man's relation to God. As a wife, woman is contained and controlled by the husband. To undermine any residual notions that women are creators of life, Augustine claims that as mothers, women are mere instruments of God's creative power. He bestows reason and intelligence on Adam, though they are not mentioned in Genesis, and asserts that men are superior to women, who do not share these qualities. He presents Eve as a foolish woman, solely responsible for the Fall and expulsion from Eden. Even though Adam also ate the fruit, Augustine explains that he sinned with his eyes open – he was not deceived. Eve beguiled him with her sexual charms to the point where he could not continue to obey God's commandment. Augustine offers this interpretation as an illustration of how women are dangerous to men and need to be contained and controlled (Agonito: Augustine).

Male superiority and dominance over women continuously required reinforcement through stories, especially during times of great social upheaval. During the plagues of the Middle Ages, the Catholic Church controlled explanations for scientific and medical phenomena, and claimed the plague was both allowed by God to punish people, and also brought on by witches in league with the Devil who wanted to destroy Christianity. The printing press had just been invented, and while the Bible was the first book printed and distributed widely, *The Malleus Maleficarum* – The Hammer of Witches – was printed in equal number. Written by two Catholic priests, this became the handbook to guide priests everywhere on how to identify a witch, interrogate a witch, and kill a witch. The Malleus identified witches as almost always women, an accusation anchored to entrenched male views of women. The authors explain that women are weaker mentally and morally, more impressionable, so easier to be drawn in by the Devil (Kramer, 44). But fears about witches concerned more than the destruction of Christianity; they centered on fertility, pregnancy, and childbirth. The power of the Devil over women was anchored to Eve succumbing to the temptation of the serpent (as Satan) to eat the fruit, which by the 13th century had become firmly understood as unbridled and immoral lust. The Malleus explains that women are more carnal than men, a trait passed down from Eve, and lust "in women is insatiable" (Kramer, 47). Kramer held that through their powers of seducing men, women could use the act of generation to cause social havoc either through causing inordinate lust in men or complete impotence. Witches were thought to cast spells preventing men from ejaculating, making them incapable of engendering children. Men feared witches could actually steal penises (Kramer, 47, 52, 56). Worse, women could prevent pregnancy, cause miscarriages, or perform abortions. If they could not succeed in aborting the fetus, midwives would give the baby to the Devil (Kramer, 66). Male distrust in women's ability to control pregnancy and to deliver babies grew. Witches came to represent a political, religious and sexual threat to Protestant and Catholic churches, as well as the State between the 13th and 17th centuries.

The original doctors in Western culture were women healers. The rise to dominance of male professionals was NOT a natural process, nor the result of women's failure to take on healing work. A struggle for control of the medical profession, based on politics, religion, gender, and class, began with the suppression and destruction of women healers as witches, and led to the rise of medical schools for men and the outlawing of midwives. Political and economic monopolization of medicine meant control over its institutional organizations, its theories and practices, its profits and prestige in ways that reinforced patriarchy (Ehrenreich, 4).

Medicine as a profession required university training, making it easy to bar women legally. Laws were established to prohibit all but university-trained doctors from practicing medicine. Led by non-surgical barber-surgeons, by the 17th and 18th centuries, men made inroads into the field of obstetrics, which became a lucrative business. Male doctors were taught to treat by heroic measures – massive bleeding, huge doses of laxatives, and opium – which were deemed safer and more effective than herbs and techniques used by women healers, especially midwives. By 1830, 13 states in America had passed medicinal licensing laws outlawing female healers, who were cast as ignorant and dirty (Ehrenreich, 34). Such laws resulted in male control over female bodies, pregnancies, and childbirth, which led to further legal acts making birth control and abortion illegal.

And here we are.

A MODEST PROPOSAL

The right to determine if and when to have children was a very long battle, one most people thought was won and over. The overturning of Roe has thrown women back 50 years and propped up patriarchal power. If Republicans succeed in creating a nationwide ban on abortions, the lives of many people will be negatively affected in ways not given appropriate concern or consideration. Thousands of women will be forced to carry fetuses with severe illnesses or birth defects, or give birth to babies created through abuse, rape, or incest. Thousands of women will have their education and/or career goals interrupted or totally derailed; more will lose out on promotions, raises, and bonuses. Hundreds of thousands of women will fall into poverty. Those women who become poor and without the means to take care of their children will reap the scorn of those who claim women shouldn't have babies if they can't afford to raise them. If those women are unmarried, they will be slut-shamed and blamed for their own circumstances. Through lack of opportunity in careers and education, a life in poverty consumed with the constant work of mere survival, and the social shaming of women who did not go about marrying and creating a family "the right (moral) way", women will be contained in the subordinate position, either suffering difficult lives or economically dependent on others for help. Male dominance and the patriarchal power structures will be reinforced.

Caveat: Patriarchy is not men. Patriarchy is a system formed around the interpretation of difference using concepts about gender that create inequality that privileges the group "men" and grants them dominance over the group "women". The system is then reinforced through the dominant stories crafted and circulated through the institutions of religion and law and science, which shape the beliefs and actions of people. There are plenty of women who also reinforce patriarchal social structures and power systems, as evident in the Right to Life organizations and political movement, or everyday slut-shaming. Some of those women benefit from whatever power is held by men with whom they are associated. But it is generally (white, straight, Christian) men who reap most of the positions of power and authority, and most of the wealth.

It will take many years of people fighting through politics and the legal system to regain complete autonomy and control over their bodies and lives. So if those who can get pregnant are forced to relinquish their bodies for nine months, some demands must be met.

1. Anyone who becomes pregnant should receive free housing, pre-natal health care, delivery in hospital, and a guarantee they will still have their job after giving birth.

2. Anyone forced to give birth has the legal right of first refusal. In other words, the birth-giver can opt out of taking the baby home, or raising that child. In these cases, the person who impregnated them will have full responsibility to house, feed, and care for that child, and to provide health care. That person will arrange and pay for every doctor visit, and all needs for childcare and education. That person will be expected to raise that child, lovingly and with discipline, so that baby becomes a responsible and productive citizen of this country.

3. If the birth-giver decides to take the baby home from the hospital, they must receive societal and economic support to house, feed, educate, and care for that child if needed.

4. Because the catalyst for the legal demand that those with wombs be held hostage to their reproductive capabilities because of a belief that life is sacred, any person who impregnates someone and then murders them to avoid economic responsibilities or disruptions in their life goals and desires shall receive the death penalty for killing two people – the carrier and the baby.

Nota Bene: This proposed solution is oversimplified and impossible to actually create. It is satirical and meant to evoke reflection and spark discussion and creative problem solving. It is also meant to encourage people to unite and fight politically for bodily autonomy.

Works Cited

Agonito, Rosemary. "Woman as Auxiliary and Subject to Man." *History of Ideas on Women*. Paragon. 1977. Pp. 74 – 78.

Black Maternal Health Momnibus Act of 2021, 117th Congress (2021 – 2022). H.R. 959.

Durkee, Alison. "Even Most Republicans Don't Want Congress to Ban Abortion Nationwide." *Forbes*, May 9, 2022.

Ehrenreich, Barbara and English, Deirdre. *Witches, Midwives, and Nurses: A History of Women Healers*. The Feminist Press of the City University of New York, 1973.

Finer, Lawrence B., Frohwirth, Lori F., Dauphinee, Lindsay, and Moore, Ann. "Reasons U.S. Women Have Abortions: Quantitative and Qualitative Perspectives." *Perspectives on Sexual and Reproductive Health: A Journal of Peer Reviewed Research*, Guttmacher Institute, September 1, 2005.

French, Marilyn. *From Eve to Dawn; a History of Women in the World. Volume One: Origins*. The Feminine Press at the City University of New York. 2008.

Graham, Elizabeth. The Ethics and Religious Liberty Commission of the Southern Baptist Convention. *Why we aim to make abortion illegal, unthinkable, and unnecessary.* June 14, 2022.

"Herschel Walker's Son Goes OFF on His Father." YouTube. Oct. 4, 2022.

Human Life International. "Empowering You to Build a Pro-Life, Pro-Family World" May 5, 2021.

Jacobovic, Simcha. "Biblical Femme Fatale Jezebel! – The Naked Archeologist 116 – Jezebel Bible Bad Girl." *Naked Archeologist*. March 20, 2019.

"Joan Chittister on the Meaning of Pro-Life." *Interview with Bill Moyer*. 2004.

King, Maya, Lerer, Lisa, and Bromwich, Jonah. "Herschel Walker Urged Woman to Have a 2nd Abortion, She Says." *The New York Times*. Oct. 7, 2022.

Kramer, Heinrich, and Spencer, James. *The Malleus Maleficarum*. Translated by Rev. Montague Summers. Dover Publications, 1971.

Levine, Jeff. "No. 1 Cause of Death in Pregnant Women: Murder." *Web MD*; *Journal of American Medical Association,* March 20. 2001.

National Constitution Center. *Supreme Court Case 597 U. S. Dobbs v. Jackson Women's Health Organization*, 2022.

"South Carolina Republican Senator Katrina Shealy Responds, Pointing a Lack of Republican Support for Bills That Would Help Mothers and Children." *Yahoo News*.

The Holy Bible; King James Version. American Bible Society, n. d.

Wallace, Maeve PhD; Gillispie-Bell, Veronica MD; Cruz, Kiara MPH; Davis, Kelly MPA; Vilda, Dovile PhD. "Homicide During Pregnancy and the Postpartum Period in the States, 2018 – 2019." *Obstetrics & Gynecology*. Vol. 138, no. 5. November 2021. Pp. 762 – 769.

The Empty Womb

Liz Darling

Grin and Childbear It

Allison Fradkin

Once upon a time,
the platitude was:
Beggars can't be choosers.
Today we're Wade-ing into the attitude:
Eggers can't be choosers.
Why not let her be?
Why take the letter B,
the A for autonomy,
the C for choice?
It's bad enough that you
deemphasize and
dehumanize her.
Must you
de-alphabetize her as well?
But then, the ball is no longer
in her court
It's being bounced on
fertile ground
and hapless hips.
Because the Supremes' baby love
has given her the shaft
and the bundle of joy
its reception may result in.

I can just hear the majority humming
your infantilizing victory song
as they over-the-moonwalk on air:
Breed it, just breed it.
Well, she doesn't have to be
Janet Jackson
to take control,
so you can beat it
like Michael would roll.

It's really that simple.
Because when you take the pro
out of reproductive
you get reductive.
So you may not want to
rejoice yet.
Because she's going to
re-choice yet
again.
Her fight's not over.
It's ovaried.
Dissatisfied with your
vote-by-*male* system,
she's not only planning to
rock the boat.
She's planning to
Roe it.
As a matter of fact,
she's giving birth
to the totally
fallopian
tubular
concept
that yes, she can
uterise up
and take you down.
You must
support that babe
up in arms.
After all, you believe that
life begins
at conception,
right?

Conjure Woman
Reda Rackley aka Bonewoman

Conjure Woman Ain't Messing Around

Reda Rackley aka Bonewoman

make no bones about it, conjure woman ain't fuckin around!
she'll put a spell on you... before you even know what went down!
she don't mess around with no shuck & jive,
she's all about keepin a woman alive!
you hurt a woman's body & soul
she'll have you diggin your very own hole.
she'll throw you in;
bury your bones
dance on your grave,
she always has the final say!
Men in black robes think they won
their troubles just begun!
Her daughters rising one by one
A mighty force brighter than the sun.
The fires are hot the fires are holy
A woman's womb is her glory!
We will fight to the death
We will fight to the end
We are tired of dead old white men
Time for the old sick kings to die
The Fierce Feminine She Rise She Rise!

Moving Worlds
Arna Baartz

Bodily Autonomy and Sovereignty through a Sex Education Curriculum of Self Pleasure

Kay Louise Aldred

Sex education centres the female body as a resource for the penetrative experience of the heterosexual male.

It is inherently patriarchal, misogynist (the female body submits to the male's), oppressive and heteronormative (sex is done one way – penis in vagina) and sexist (no mention of female gratification – the focus is on the male orgasm).

At least this is the case in the UK – where I taught adolescents for almost two decades.

Sex education does not educate young women in self-ownership of autonomous sexual desire and satisfaction. It does not teach, in any detail, about the clitoris, self-pleasure, female orgasm and the wellbeing, empowerment and self-confidence benefits of sexual curiosity, self-exploration and masturbation.

Girls are not taught about the power, sacredness and magic of their sexuality. They are not educated to embrace solo sexual self-pleasure – bodily autonomy – to fill themselves up first. Neither do they receive tutelage in the joy of self-orgasm – to get to know what their body loves – to discern their yes and no in terms of sexual preferences, touch and activity.

The task of a liberation theology of embodiment and Goddess Spirituality is to address this; to speak on behalf of the oppressed – in this case girls and the female body – which are, of course, Goddess.

I stand for teaching girls to sexually self-explore and get to know themselves and what their body desires – their likes and dislikes. I stand for teaching girls to pleasure themselves to such an extent that they delight and fully own the sovereignty, power and sacredness of their own body and sexuality. That they can meet and fulfill their own sexual needs to such an extent that they won't settle for anything less in a sexual partner in terms of respect, reverence and gratification than that which they can give to themselves.

I stand for bodily autonomy and sovereignty through a sex education curriculum of self-pleasure.

Sycamore Fig

Annelinde Metzner

I know you by your absence, my adoration,
  your familiarity.
Great tree, Ficus Sycomorus, twenty meters tall,
  twice that in width,
  reaching out your wide expanse to protect us,
  our Ancient Mother.
Asherah! Asherah! I remember you as Goddess,
  nurturing us, fostering all beings,
  and in that life, in that dream,
  You were our altar.
Heart-shaped leaves, a canvas for artists through the ages.
Your abundant fruits! Flowering year-long,
  they ripen green to yellow to richest red,
  proof of your divinity.
Each fruit-fall, a ton, ripens at Your leisure,
  at all times of the year, as it pleases You.
When You, Asherah, were Goddess at our altar,
  were those thousands of rich red fruits
  all the proof we needed?
At our altars, two thousand years ago and so much more,
  You fed us all, monkeys and humans, elephants and bats.
In Egypt, they painted You everywhere,
  as we suckled at Your holy breasts.
"Destroy their altar, break their images,
  and cut down their Asherim!"
  cried Moses, the teachings of the advancing hoards
  echoing down through the ages.
The good red fruit, Your menstrual blood,
  Your woman-power, Your all-giving grace,
  Your place of honor by the altar
  is now lost to us all.
Oh our Mother! Asherah! Sycamore Fig!

I am there again, singing,
    with my sistrum and my drum,
    dancing with all my people
    to the beat of the tambourine.
Roots wide-spread underground, Your massive canopy overhead,
    I feel You reverberating,
    happy under our feet as we dance.
Oh Asherah, Sycamore Fig! African Queen,
    Queen of Trees, beloved of Egypt,
    adored in the Holy Land,
    in those holiest days before Yahweh and his swordsmen
    set out to destroy You...
You fed us all.
I feel Your wide-splayed roots
    and your luscious wide canopy
    growing holy and happy once more,
    fruits as red as my blood,
    in the ageless and undying altar of my heart.

Wombniverse / The Red Sea

Liz Darling

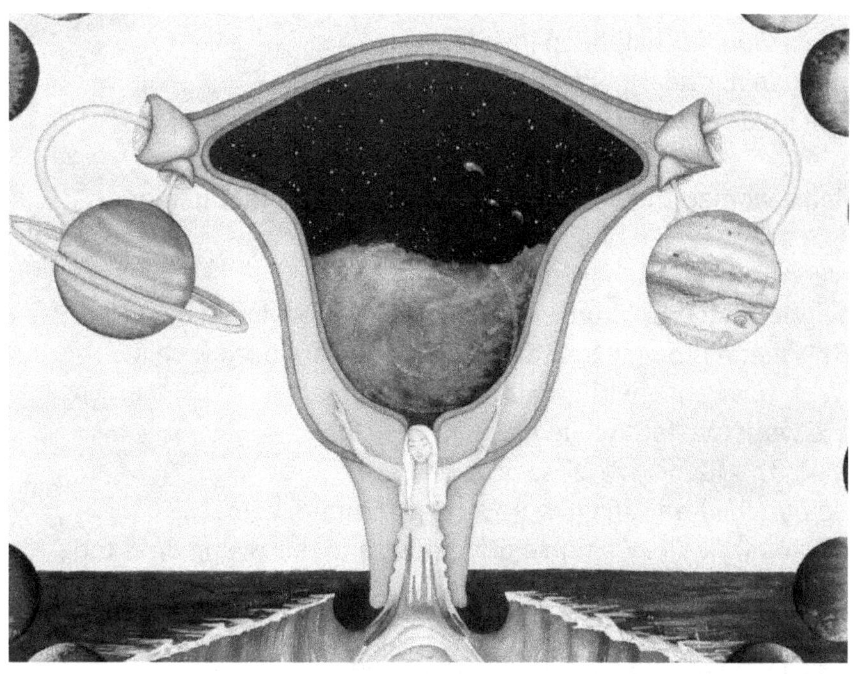

Tell a Woman

Annelinde Metzner

Tell a woman that, deep inside,
deep in her heart, where no one can see,
she holds the flame that lights the world.

Tell a woman that no one can ever extinguish that flame.
Not anyone, be he bigger than her,
stronger than her, faster than her,
angrier than her, drunker than her, more convinced he is right.
This flame is our secret, all women's. We are born with it.
With this flame, within our hearts,
we work two jobs while raising three kids.
With this flame, we cross oceans
so our children can grow up strong without stigma.
With this flame, we nurse our elders, and our young ones too,
often at the same time, scrounging for food and rent.

Tell a woman she has a huge bright flame
ready to flare up in her heart,
and she's not alone. We all have one,
we who walk tall, and we who are under the thumb,
we who speak now, and we who have been silenced,
we all share this flame, it's an eternal flame.

Tell a woman, this is our birthright, this is who we are,
we, the women, the people of the womb
who carry the world, who yearn for love and honor,
who, somewhere deep inside, will never be denied,
will never give in.

Tell a woman, this is who we are,
all of us carrying that precious fire
that shows us its light and tells us how to move,
how to be, how to turn, how to love each day.

Tell a woman, she has a pure flame deep in her heart
that can never be extinguished, that cannot be pushed under,
that can only rise higher, that flares up within us,
and with each step brightens, and lights our way
more clearly, more loudly, more assuredly, more proudly,
all of us gazing at that brand new day,
not much longer now, just on the horizon,
when we look at a woman and know,
with her light, she leads the way.

The Coming of Lilith

Arlene Bailey

Shifting Sands

Arlene Bailey

While they were out celebrating
Raising their glasses to the
Erect god between their legs
We shed our tears, spoke our rage
And then we began to mobilize

Never think you can best a woman
For we have had years to learn your
Ways of thinking and acting and
We will not go backwards

EVEN
IF
THAT

Is the only direction YOU know

We WILL sharpen our swords,
Our brains and with the
Fierceness of Kali,
Ferocity of Sekhmet,
Screech of Lilith and the
Sword of Boudicca,
We will once again triumph

With the wit and wisdom of
An' Morrighan and the
Magic of the Great Mother,
Along with the Holy Rage of
Every woman on this planet,
As well as those still yet to come

And those who dwell in other
Worlds and realms...

Hear this and take heed!

We will NOT go gently into that
Proverbial good night[22], for we have
Put up with your ways and rage
For millennia and we have learned
Well your mind as you have

BURNED US!

DROWNED US!

TORTURED US!

And attempted via
Law and Religion to
CONTROL US!

BUT. HEAR. THIS!

Just as your time and
your ways had a beginning,
they also have an ending

There's a timer on your actions

And the sands

Are

Already

Shifting

---

[22] *Paraphrase of Dylan Thomas' poem.

Lilith

Arna Baartz

A Call to the Goddesses, A Call to My Sisters

Renee Bedard

The news came down like a weight upon me. It simply took my breath away. I could feel the collective scream of all the women in our country and those who came before us cry out at the same time. It felt like a dream. I was bombarded with rapid waves of emotions that took me down into a very dark place. Shock. Fear. Sadness. Confusion. Rage. They all kept coming in different patterns and intensity. I had no words to express what I was feeling. I didn't know what to do. I couldn't find a shred of hope inside me, let alone figure out what I could do to help change this drastic ruling. I knew intellectually that Roe had a thin chance for survival. Like many, I clung to the hope that the law for the last fifty years would stand for something. Yet when the decision was made public, I felt everything change in that instant. The hard truth is, our lives did change that day. The ruling threw us back into the uncertainty of the past, stripping away our right to control our own bodies and our lives once more.

When I am unsure of what to do in a situation or in the aftermath of a difficult or life changing experience, I look to the myths and stories of the Goddesses and powerful women that empower and inspire me. I feel that these tales can offer us a roadmap on how to overcome the setbacks and closed doors we face today, leaving us feeling powerless and alone. Women have struggled for so many years. We endure the same struggles as those in the myths and legends of old. That is why I look to myth and story. We can look to Goddesses like The Morrigan, Macha, and Medb.

Goddesses that stand for sovereignty and autonomy and will not be torn asunder. We have Medusa who had suffered deeply and Lilith who was demonized. Their stories hold a deep and transformative power. They show us how we can claim our own unique ability to shift, adapt, and evolve. Athena's wisdom can give us insight into ways of strategy and planning. Boudicca was a fierce leader who raised an army against the Holy Roman Empire and would not shrink from or abandon her principles. While it is true that every story does not have a happy ending, these women embody strength, tenacity, and divine spirit. Their myths and stories are our stories. Their battles and hardships are ours as well. They faced what appeared to be an impenetrable wall that would prevent their success. Yes, some of their battles were lost. However, their stories live on. They live on through us in our bones, blood, and spirit. We still struggle with the same issues as our great-great-grandmothers. As a woman, I can feel them with me. As a witch, I know they are there. Walking with us, they cheer us on. For we are their dreams made manifest and we have the power together to create the change we wish to see in the world.

I wrote this prayer the weekend after Roe was taken down. This is how I choose to begin my work in order to prepare myself for the real-world action I must take. Light a candle and let your voice be heard.

A Prayer to the Sovereigns

We stand together and raise our voice,
United in our call.
Together we stand for Liberty and Justice for all.

By The Morrigan –
May we shift and change as we commit to this enduring battle.
Our sovereignty is what we claim.
We will not be dismissed or treated as cattle.

By Macha's foresight and fiery will,
may we strategize and embrace our cunning.
Our bodies, our own.
Our lives, our own.
Without mercy, we curse those who send us running.

In full power, we call to Medb and embrace our divine spirit.
A natural force.
A commanding force.
We will not be ashamed of our power, sexuality, or bodies.

By Medusa's piercing and stony stare,
We reclaim our power, body, and story.
May we shatter all that holds us back,
As we rise from the dust towards our glory.

With Lilith's courage and confidence, we will not be put asunder.
We claim our sex.
We claim our life.
We will not be suppressed by another.

By Athena's power to strategize,
may our plans be precise and wise.
May our paths be clear,
Messages held dear,
For we shall have final say in our lives.

By Boudicca's sword and protective shield,
may we defeat the grotesque and defiling hoards.
Hate and discrimination will not stand.
Our Liberty we race towards.

Morrigan. Macha. Medb. Medusa. Lilith. Athena. Boudicca.
Feel our hearts.
Hear our cries.
Join us as we stand for what is right.
Gird us as we walk our path, uncertain of what lurks this night.

Be with us.
Fortify us.
For there is much work to be done.
Love is love.
Our body, our choice.

Only we know who we are inside.
May we be free, sovereign, and unafraid, with the power to decide.
By Law. By Light. By Life. By Love.
We claim our divine Liberty.
On this day, we raise our spirits,
Together we form perfect unity.

Implant this prayer upon our hallowed ground,
Let us feel it in our bones.
May we walk this path strong and proud,
Straight into the unknown.

Stand with us as we raise our voices, strengthening our call.
May the corrupt and vile policies break.
May the weight of tyranny burn and fall.

* * * * * * * *

Yes, it is true. Women have endured repression for millennia. Our voices and stories have been silenced and ignored. We also have voices and stories that have rattled and broken the chains that once bound us. Look to them. Hear their words. Feel their strength and power. Welcome their love, acceptance, and wisdom. Know that our sovereign sisters and Goddesses walk with us every day. Their words and deeds echo through time. Let them feed you. Let them lift you. Let their success, strength, and courage carry you when you feel low, confused, and afraid. Remember, we are the ones whom we have been waiting for and together we have a collective spirit with incredible fortitude and immense love. Let this be our fuel. This is the call of the Goddesses. This is the call of our sisters.

Medusa's Scream

Claire Dorey

The Howl of Ages

Mary Saracino

A woman's fury is blood deep
bone strong,
uterine fierce,
unstoppable.
No man can tame it
though many have tried.
We must unleash the howl of ages,
uncoil our collective memory,
proclaim our authority to self-rule,
reclaim what has been erased, denied
stolen from our remembering mother tongues.
We must call down our midnight powers,
put a hex on them, cast a spell
condemn their vile hubris that seeks
to dismember female sovereignty.
We must undo this horrific undoing
heed the wailing of our mothers
our grandmothers, our great-greats
far back into antiquity,
the ones they burned and tortured
the ones they killed in the name of uncivil civilization.
We must light the torch of resistance,
let loose our chilling battle cry,
fight, again, and again, and again
to overthrow this cruel and brutal
attempt to eviscerate
all that is innately, inextricably ours.
With every fiber of our endangered wombs
we must rage, rage
against this assault on all that is female, inviolable, sacred.

Rise up, sisters. Resist!
For our mothers and grandmothers,
our daughters and granddaughters,
for ourselves.

Boudicca Rising

Barbara O'Meara

Laughter

Amy Barron Smolinski

She moved
quietly with practiced steps
through the world men built.
Her smile
was her passport
sometimes her shield
sometimes her weapon
always her currency
bestowed as a reward for an overvalued act of kindness
or to soften a request
that is really a demand.

But in the solace
of the world that women
carve out in underground nooks
and crannies
in tree roots and caves and warm warrens
and kitchen tables
and idling cars,
the glamour of her smile left on the dresser with
her discarded underwire bra
and strand of pearls,

She laughed
with her friends,
their laughter no longer bound by the constraints of the world
men built.

They cackled
loudly
their raucous joy bubbling up from
their loosened and round bellies
punctuated by snorts of delight
appreciative chuckles
and hearty guffaws of high amusement
and profound depths
ending often in cleansing tears.

In the world of men
whose delicate ears and egos fear
loud noises
and feelings
the laugher of women must be quiet
tinkling
giggling
polite
and fit into a very narrow spectrum of decibels.

But
in the sanctuary of women
the laughter of crones is thunderous
with the power to destroy worlds
and build new ones.

Enrealment

Kat Shaw

Sovereign Wombs

Melisa Ann Howarth

This is MY sacred vessel; my temple of divinity.
I govern it alone, as such.
Great Spirit has bestowed this right upon us all.
I am the protector of this portal;
You have no say or rights here.
I stand for the sovereignty of all wombs.
I stand for the sanctity of all that it means
to be born of this flesh.
Those who dare try to tread upon it,
shall be met with the unstoppable will
of Divine Feminine power;
for the blood of the ancestral Mothers still flows through us all.

Women of the World Unite

Cheryl Braganza

"This painting envisions a future where women of all colors and cultures join hands to collectively effect positive change in the world. Where, by uniting with other women, they feel free: free to challenge and break boundaries, to empower other women, to make their own choices, to walk the streets unthreatened and to bring a new sense of peace and justice. The power of women is unmistakable as they gather momentum, finally recognize their true potential and rise up in revolution to effect real change around the world." -Cheryl Braganza

When Sleeping Women Waken

Trista Hendren

We began this anthology with outrage over the reversal of Roe v. Wade—but I did not know how to end it.

The contributors did such a tremendous job of weaving this compilation together that it seemed there was nothing left for me to say. And yet, I felt compelled to share a few final thoughts...

Sovereignty begins at birth. We are all born supreme beings. I saw this clearly with my children. They came into this world filled with Divine Wisdom. I vowed that I would never squash that.

Watching my children grow up illuminated all of the ways I was not allowed to be autonomous in my own life. I was groomed to be the quiet, submissive girl who did exactly what she was told. This ultimately made me a target for sexual abuse, attempted rape—and physical, emotional, and financial abuse—primarily by men who claimed to love me.

It is time to stop giving tyrannical men any of our time, energy, or resources.

Men who take these things by force must finally meet the full brunt of the consequences.

The saturation of Innocent children in patriarchal religions must end. There is no justification for poisoning our children in the same toxicity we nearly drowned in.

We must continue to actively deconstruct our own upbringings so that we can heal.

Our bodies are our own, first and foremost. But—by patriarchal design—many of us know very little about them.

We must learn everything we can about our bodies—and teach our daughters and granddaughters about theirs. We need to remember how to treasure our bodies—and nurture them with love. Sovereignty resides here.

Patriarchy wears us down. We are all exhausted from the day-to-day grind of living under a capitalist system that favors white men. We are underpaid, overworked, and under-appreciated. Worse, our bodies have been subjugated, abused, and raped—often from a very young age.

It took me a very long time as a sexual abuse survivor to begin to have any idea what bodily autonomy even meant. I have grown stronger with each reclamation of my being. Beau Taplin wrote:

> "Listen to me, your body is not a temple. Temples can be destroyed and desecrated. Your body is a forest—thick canopies of maple trees and sweet scented wildflowers sprouting in the underwood. You will grow back, over and over, no matter how badly you are devastated."

We must create our own forests of women deeply rooted in their own sovereignty.

Creating a new world order is no small task. But each of us can create our own spheres—our own matriarchal households where *we* decide how things are run.

Never forget that your grandmothers are guiding you, demanding freedom from the shackles they were imprisoned with.

May we heal our ancestral lines, bringing forth liberation for women and girls throughout the world.

The mountains have begun moving—but that is not enough. We need more women to awaken and join us.

Ursula le Guin wrote: "We are volcanoes. When we women offer our experience as our truth, all the maps change. There are new mountains."[23]

The treacherous mountains of patriarchy must collapse. It is time for the ancient mountains of the Great Mother to re-emerge.

---

[23] Le Guin, Ursula K. from her 1986 Bryn Mawr commencement speech, reprinted in *Dancing at the Edge of the World*. Grove Press; 1997.

List of Contributors

Allison Fradkin (she/her/hers) delights in applying her Women's & Gender Studies education to the creation of satirically scintillating poetry, prose, and plays that (sur)pass the Bechdel Test and enlist their characters in a caricature of the idiocies and intricacies of insidious isms. Fradkin freelances for her hometown of Chicago as Co-Artistic Director and Literary Manager of Violet Surprise Theatre, curating new works by queer women. Allison's auxiliary activities include vintage shopping, volunteering, and tending to her thespian tendencies.

Amy Barron Smolinski holds an MA from Union Institute and University, where she focused on Goddess Studies under the late Patricia Monaghan. She is an initiate in the Ifa tradition to the priesthood of Obatala, and an internationally recognized expert on support and advocacy for breastfeeding military families, as well as an actress, director, and audio book narrator. She lives in Germany with her husband and four sons, where she serves as Managing Artistic Director of KMC Onstage, an American military community theatre.

Andrea Redmond has been a feminist rights activist, artist and pagan for over 50 years. She has been a devotee of The Morrigan since a young girl.

She was born on Prince Edward Island, Canada of Irish descent and moved to Ireland with her young family and there, she was one of the first women in Belfast to paint wall murals. Her first mural in 1983 honoured womens rights activists from Ireland and South Africa. She has painted over 40 murals with similar themes and her work has been featured in a number of publications and films on Northern Ireland.

She has worked and chaired a number of women's, art and multicultural groups. She has taught programs in art, community development and youth work. She is a mother to three children and returned to education in her 40s, completing her PhD, at the University of Ulster.

Andrea currently resides in rural Donegal, Ireland where she operates her art studio / workshop. Her artwork is in permanent collections and galleries in Ireland, Canada and the United States.

Anna Begas is an inspired healer, body worker, and women´s coach. She has been working with women for 10+ years, in private, on retreats, in countless women's circles and online. She is a creative soul, a traveler and rebel by heart, and a mother of 2!
She works with sensitive souls in guiding them to shine their light out into the world by taking their full space, and connecting deeply to the alive and en-spirited natural world for support.

Anna is Dutch, but left the Netherlands when she was 18, and lived a nomadic life around the world for over 10 years. Since having children, she has become more settled and has been living in the South of Spain for another 10+ years now.

Annelinde Metzner is a poet and composer living in the Blue Ridge Mountains of North Carolina, who is devoted to the return of the Goddess through her art and lifework. She directs the women's choir Sahara Peace Choir and founded Womansong of Asheville. Annelinde produces concerts of her poetry and music and is working on some art songs for solo soprano using her own and ancient texts for the Goddess. See more of her work at AnnelindesWorld.blogspot.com.

Poet, performer, and teacher **Annie Finch** is the author of a dozen books, including *The Poetry Witch Little Book of Spells, Eve, A Poet's Craft*, and the epic poem on abortion *Among the Goddesses*, which received the Sarasvati Award from ASWM. Her eight edited books include *Choice Words: Writers on Abortion*, the first major literary anthology on abortion. She holds a Ph.D. from Stanford University and descends from witches imprisoned in the Salem Witch Trials. Annie has taught widely and performs through Poetry Witch Ritual Theater.

She teaches classes in poetry, meter, witchery, and her original transformative teaching, The Magic of Rhythmically Writing, at PoetryWitchCommunity.org. You can find Annie on Twitter: @poetrywitch and Instagram: @thepoetrywitch.

C. Ara Campbell is a visionary writer, author of the book *Dark Goddess Magick*, and founder of *The Goddess Circle*. She is a soul-guide, cosmic channel, facilitator of *The Inner Priestess Awakening Online Journey* and *Relationship Empowerment & Sacred Love Online Journey,* and author of *The Astro Forecast Publication*. She is a contributing author on *Journeys with the Divine Feminine, Original Resistance: Reclaiming Lilith, Reclaiming Ourselves*, and upcoming *Kali Rising, Holy Rage.* Ara is a modern-day mystic dedicated to empowering others, connecting them with their purpose, living embodied truth and healing using the natural world. Ara is an old soul that has been writing and channeling guidance from the unseen since she was young, intuitively soul coaching using spiritual and natural energies. She can often be found seeking wisdom and solace in the wilds of Mother Earth, capturing the magic of nature with her camera, or snuggling her dog, Sonny.

Arlene Bailey is a visionary artist and author on the quest of "woman know thyself". Working in the realm of the Sacred Wild Woman in all her many visages, her paintings, poetry and prose reflect the raw, visceral and innate wild in all women, while also challenging and questioning everything we know to be true about the who of who we are as women walking in this time.

Through her magical weavings in word and paint and, drawing on her trainings and skills as an Ordained Priestess, Women's Mysteries Facilitator, Wise Woman Herbalist, Energy Medicine Practitioner and Retired Anthropologist (M.A.), Arlene invites women to step into personal sovereignty as they listen to their ancient memories and voice of their soul.

Published in nine Girl God anthologies, Arlene is also a monthly contributor for Return to Mago E-Magazine and is published in *She Summons: Why Goddess Feminism, Activism and Spirituality,* 2021 by Mago Publications. She is also a contributor to the 2024 *We'Moon Calendar* in addition to the upcoming Mago anthology *Celebrating Intercosmic Kinship of the Goddess* (Publication TBA).

Along with her three cats, this Wild Crone lives deep in the ancient Appalachian Mountains of North Carolina, USA. Currently, she is working on a book of her own art, poetry and prose.

Find her work below…

www.hersacredwild.com
www.facebook.com/hersacredwild/
www.thegirlgod.com
ww.magobooks.com
www.magoism.net

Arna Baartz is a painter, writer/poet, martial artist, educator and mother to eight fantastic children. She has been expressing herself creatively for more than 40 years and finds it to be her favourite way of exploring her inner being enough to evolve positively in an externally-focused world. Arna's artistic and literary expression is her creative perspective of the stories she observes playing out around her. Claims to fame: Arna has been selected for major art prizes and won a number of awards, published many books, and— (her favourite) was being used as a 'paintbrush' at the age of two by well-known Australian artist John Olsen. Arna lives and works from her bush studio in the Northern Rivers, NSW Australia. Her website is www.artofkundalini.com

Bambi Lobdell received her PhD in English from Binghamton University in 2007. Bambi taught at SUNY Oneonta for over 21 years and developed many classes for the Women's and Gender Studies departments, including Women of Resistance; Witches, Harlots, and Wild Women; Queer Literature; Transgender Studies; Gender, Race, and Sexuality in Memoir; and American Masculinities. Her dissertation research on her ancestor, Lucy Ann/Joseph Israel Lobdell resulted in the book *A Strange Sort of Being* (MacFarland, 2012), the detailed biography of Lucy/Joe Lobdell's life, analyzed with gender and queer theories and embedded in historical discussions. She has presented on Lucy/Joe at numerous conferences and has been interviewed by *The Advocate magazine, Philadelphia Gay News,* and *The Washington Post.* Bambi is dedicated to educating people on feminist and transgender issues.

Barbara O'Meara, professional visual artist, art activist, published writer & co-editor of 'Soul Seers Irish Anthology of Celtic Shamanism'. Her 20 Solo Exhibitions include 'B.O.R.N.Babies of Ravaged Nations'. International juried shows include ASWM 'Wisdom Across the Ages', Lockhart Gallery New York 'Contemporary Irish Art' & Herstory 'Brigid's of the World' & 'Black Lives Matter'. Community Arts include 'Stitched With Love' Tuam Baby Blanket laid out onsite at the Mother & Child Institution by survivors and families, at KOLO International Women's Non Killing Cross Borders Summit in Sarajevo and held by Bosnian women war survivors. 'Sort Our Smears' Campaign at 'Festival of FeminismS'. 'Home Words Bound' publication with National Collective of Community Based Women's Networks where her paintings accompany writing by Irish women about the Pandemic. She is continually developing empowering women's 'Art as Activism' projects. She is honoured to be included in several Girl God Books, including being the featured artist of a new publication, *My Name is Brigid* which launched on Brigid's Day 2022.

Website: www.barbaraomearaartist.com

H. Byron Ballard, BA, MFA, is a western NC native, teacher, folklorist and writer. She has served as a featured speaker and teacher at Sacred Space Conference, Summerland Spirit Festival, Pagan Spirit Gathering, Southeast Wise Women's Herbal Conference, Glastonbury Goddess Conference, Heartland, Sirius Rising, Starwood, Scottish Pagan Federation Conference and other gatherings. She is senior priestess and co-founder of Mother Grove Goddess Temple and the Coalition of Earth Religions/CERES, both in Asheville, NC.

Her essays are featured in several anthologies and she writes a regular column for *Witches and Pagans* Magazine. Her book *Staubs and Ditchwater* debuted in 2012 and the companion volume *Asfidity and Mad-Stones* was published in Oct. 2015. *Embracing Willendorf: A Witch's Way of Loving Your Body to Health and Fitness* launched in May, 2017. *Earth Works: Ceremonies in Tower Time* debuted in June 2018. Byron is currently at work on *Gnarled Talisman: Old Wild Magics of the Motherland* and *The Ragged Wound: Tending the Soul of Appalachia.*

Cheryl Braganza (February 25, 1945–December 16, 2016) was a gifted artist and poet. Of Goan origin, she was born in Bombay and grew up in Lahore where her parents owned Braganza Hotel (referenced in "Freedom at Midnight" Collins & Lapierre). After studying languages and the arts in Rome and classical piano in London, she moved to Montreal in 1966. Essentially self-taught, her subjects vary from evocative landscapes, lush florals to vibrant figures of Indian women.

She exhibited regularly and established herself as a Quebec artist with a style of her own, using brilliant color and texture to express emotion. Her work is shared with the permission of her beloved son, Miguel, who cared for her the last 13 years of her life. You can see more of her work at www.cherylbraganza.com.

***Cheryl's Story – written by her son, Miguel Da Costa Frias**
Some people leave such a ripple on the wave of humanity, that it floats us all toward one another. This was my mother. A musician with raw unbridled talent, Cheryl was offered a scholarship to Juilliard when she was sixteen. From a young age, she played the piano, the organ, the accordion, and the harmonica with equal versatility. She began to paint in her 20's and discovered that she was a gifted painter.

She was diagnosed with a bone-related cancer on her 60th birthday in 2005 and came within a hairsbreadth from death four times, only to fight her way back to life each time. For the last decade, while fighting cancer, a handwritten quote from Goethe rested on top of her easel: "Rest not. Life is sweeping by; go and dare before you die. Something mighty and sublime, leave behind to conquer time."

Little did we know how much she would take this quote to heart or put it into action.

Cheryl developed her painting talent with exponential speed. When asked why she was working so feverishly, she answered, "I'm in a race against time. I have so much to say and so much more to bring into the world…" In her last five years of life, she produced more artwork and published more writing than she produced in the previous 20 years.

In 2008, she was named Montreal's Woman of the Year for using her art as a tool to fight for women's rights all over the world. She was featured in hundreds of media worldwide and was then elected President of the prestigious Women's Art Society of Montreal, which she grew dramatically.

Her effect on people became evident in the thousands of emails she received from people she inspired across the world.

She lived longer than anyone in recorded history with myeloma cancer in the brain, and refused painkillers because she didn't want her senses affected. Her only desire was to experience every moment in living color until her very last breath. Following her last remission, limping in pain, she decided to learn jazz from scratch, started her own jazz band and played to sold out crowds in Griffintown for two years.

Our mother believed that in order to enjoy true happiness, she should live each moment as if it were her last. Yesterday will never return. Tomorrow may never happen. While we may speak of the past or of the future, the only reality we have is that of right now, the present instant.

Confronting the reality of death enabled her to blossom with unlimited creativity, courage and joy. The more broken her body became over the years, the more she painted soaring images of birds, and butterflies, and dancing women.

She was never alone, surrounded by an ever-increasing group of family and friends who grew to love her (and each other). When the cancer finally paralyzed her body, it was our turn to bring the joy to her; kidnapping her from the hospital for secret outings, regaling her with live music every day for nine months. And even then, we marvelled how she could still paint magical tapestries of colour and love with her face, her voice and her mind.

She died peacefully in her sleep after seeing her three children; her soul soaring to the beautiful places reflected in her art.

Claire Dorey
Goldsmiths: BA Hons Fine Art.
Main Employment: Journalist and Creative, UK and overseas.
Artist: Most notable group show; Pillow Talk at the Tate Modern. Included in the *Pillow Talk Book*.
Curator: 3 x grass roots SLWA exhibitions and educational events on the subject of Female Empowerment, showcasing female artists, academic speeches and local musicians. Silence Is Over – Raising awareness on violence towards women; Ex Voto – Existential Mexican Art Therapy; Heo – Female empowerment in the self-portrait.

Extra study: Suppressed Female History: History of the Goddess; Accessing Creative Wisdom; Sound and Breath Work; Reiki Master; Colour Therapy; Hand Mudras; Reflexology; Sculpture.
Teaching Workshops: Sculpture and Drawing.

Danielle Boodoo-Fortuné is an artist, writer, mother and magicmaker from Trinidad and Tobago. Her art has been exhibited in the Caribbean as well as internationally, and featured in numerous publications. Danielle is the illustrator of *Lost! A Caribbean Sea Adventure* (CaribbeanReads) and *The Jungle Outside* (HarperCollins Publishers). She has illustrated several other projects, most recently the *EarthCraft Oracle Deck* (Hay House) in 2021.

Deborah A. Meyerriecks was accepted into New York University for pre-law studies in 1987. She found herself most at home in the stacks of NYU's Bobst Library and at the beautiful and historic Mid-Manhattan Library. A combination of factors led to her withdrawing after her second semester. She was a career EMT with NYC*EMS who accepted promotion to EMS Lieutenant after the department was merged into FDNY EMS. Deborah is an Animistic Pagan and Witch who perceives all things from animals and plants to the earth herself and all of nature and weather around her to be imbued with their own spirit, energy, and lifeforce. She has contributed to 9 Girl God Books anthologies as well as self-published her own book, *Macha and the Medic*. Currently she is co-authoring an anthology titled *Living In Magick* and is preparing to host and facilitate her 4th Shadow Care Retreat. For more information you can reach her by email at WillowMoon@yahoo.com and her website: www.WillowMoonConsulting.com

Dee Mulrooney (Growler) is an Irish artist living and working in Berlin.

Raised in a working class suburb on the Northside of Dublin in a country dominated by Catholicism and the patriarchy there was little room for artistic freedom.

Dee challenges these old paradigms with her alter-ego "Growler", an 80-year-old drum banging, shamanic giant Vulva from the inner city of Dublin. Growler facilitates healing and transmutation through storytelling, song and filthy jokes. She is a shadow worker who fits straight to the heart of taboo and takes us on a journey that only one generation ago would have seen her locked up. http://deirdre-mulrooney.com/

Dr. Denise Renye is a licensed clinical psychologist, certified sexologist, consultant and holistic coach, certified yoga therapist, and psychedelic integrationist. She has specialized training in and has worked directly with people in the areas of sexuality, relationships, embodiment, states of consciousness, psychedelic integration and intimacy. She holds a Master's degree in Human Sexuality from Widener University (Philadelphia), as well as a Master's degree and a Doctoral degree in Clinical Psychology from the California Institute of Integral Studies (San Francisco). Dr. Denise is certified as a sexologist through the American College of Sexologists. She was in the first cohort to graduate from the Center for Psychedelic Therapies and Research (CPTR) at CIIS and provides psychedelic integration individually and in group settings, utilizing trauma-informed and somatics approaches. She has studied embodied spiritual practices nationally and internationally through research and experiential learning and has conducted and published research on embodied psycho-spirituality.

Gillian M.E. Alban is Associate Professor of English Literature at Istanbul Kultur University. She is the author of *The Medusa Gaze in Contemporary Women's Fiction: Petrifying, Maternal and Redemptive*, published by Cambridge Scholars Publishing in 2017, and *Melusine the Serpent Goddess in A.S. Byatt's* Possession *and in Mythology*, published by Lexington Press in 2003; she also contributed chapters to *Re-Visioning Medusa: From Monster to Divine Wisdom* and *Original Resistance: Reclaiming Lilith, Reclaiming Ourselves*, both Girl God publications. She primarily engages with women in her writings, exploring the themes of mythic women from the twenty-first to the nineteenth century, as well as writing on Shakespeare and Dystopia, elaborating her insights while enjoying the study and teaching of literature as she engages with both mythic and realistic people.

Gina Martin is a founding mother and High Priestess of Triple Spiral of Dún na Sidhe, a pagan spiritual congregation in the Hudson Valley. She is a ritualist, teacher, healer, mother, and writer of sacred songs. Her books, *When She Wakes* series (*Sisters of the Solstice Moon, Walking the Threads of Time, She Is Here*) are published by Womancraft Publishing. She is the curator and composer of *WomEnchanting: a Compendium of Sacred Songs and Chants.*

Gina is a practitioner of Classical Chinese medicine and a Board Certified licensed acupuncturist.

She lives as a steward of the land that previously held a village of the Ramapough Lenape where people can come together now to remember the Old Ways. She is kept company by her husband and dogs, as well as the Sidhe who live in the hills.

Janis Ian keeps a sign above her workspace at home, a North Star that guides her after more than five decades as a revered songwriter who dares to say what no one else will.

"Do not be held hostage by your legacy."

When you've written, starting at age 14, some of pop music's most evergreen songs — "Society's Child," "At Seventeen," "Jesse," and "Stars," among them — it's no wonder she'd need a reminder to shake free of our expectations.

Now, at 72, Ian is embracing a new milestone: the art of the farewell. Released on January 21, 2022 on her own Rude Girl Records, The Light at the End of the Line is Ian's latest and last solo studio album to bookend a kaleidoscopic catalog that began with her 1967 self-titled debut.

Jodi Blazek Gehr is a compulsive curator of images, information, and inspiration, who teaches at the same high school that she graduated from. A lifelong native of Lincoln, Nebraska, Jodi has been a business teacher for 26 years, a SoulCollage® Facilitator, Boundless Compassion Facilitator, Benedictine Oblate of Christ the King Priory, retreat leader at St. Benedict Center, and a lover of learning, reading, writing, spirituality, and creativity. She has been married to Joe for 37 years and the couple have a 28-year-old daughter, Jessica, and son-in-law, John.

Julia Jeffrey is a Scottish artist and illustrator. She studied painting at The Glasgow School of Art. Her faery and fantasy-themed work, of recent years, has attracted considerable acclaim and attention, with features in numerous international fantasy magazines. Her work appears on and in, many books and albums, and her first tarot deck, *The Tarot of the Hidden Realm*, was published in 2013.

Julie A. Dickson is a poet who addresses issues including bullying, animal and human rights, nature and environment. She advocates for captive elephants and has volunteered with feral cat rescue. Her poetry appears in many journals such as *Blue Heron, Misfit,*

Ekphrastic Review and *Deadbeat Poets*. Dickson holds a BPS in Behavioral Science and works in-home with seniors.

Kaalii Cargill is an author, artist, psychotherapist, and teacher. Her PhD explored women's reproductive autonomy through psychology, history, mythology, and anthropology:

https://trove.nla.gov.au/work/3800122 – A Phenomenological Investigation of a Psychobiological Method of Birth Control, 2000. Monash University]. Her non-fiction book – *Don't Take It Lying Down: Life According to the Goddess* – is based on her PhD research. Kaalii has published 7 books and co-edited two Mago Books anthologies: *She Rises: Why Goddess Feminism, Activism, and Spirituality, Vol 1* (2015) and *She Summons: Why Goddess Feminism, Activism, and Spirituality* (2021), both with Helen Hye-Sook Hwang. Kaalii's speculative and fantasy fiction weaves themes of mythology, Wicca, and ecofeminism.

https://kaalii.wixsite.com/soulstory

Kaalii is a mother and grandmother, currently living in the hills outside Melbourne, Australia, and travelling to ancient Goddess sites to "visit with the Grandmothers".

Karen Storminger has been a practicing polytheist pagan most of her life. Karen is a devotee of The Morrigan. She is an active member of the Connecticut Wiccan and Pagan Network and The Tuatha De Morrigan groups. She is one of the organizers and founding members of the Morrigan's Call Retreat. Karen has been writing poetry of all kinds since an early age. She has had poetry published in several anthologies: *Bibliotheca Alexandra's* Garland of the Goddess, The Dark Ones, and Girl God publication's *Warrior Queen: Answering the Call of the Morrigan*. Karen is the co-author of the book *Prayers to The Morrigan: An Illustrated Book of Devotion to the Great Queen*. You can view her blog at: https://thecrowandthedragonfly.wordpress.com/

Kat Shaw prides herself on breaking through the stereotypical views of beauty that have been cast upon society by the media, having made her name painting the glorious reality that is a woman's body.

Her nude studies of real women garnered unprecedented popularity within only a few short months, as women were crying out for themselves to be portrayed in art, rather than the airbrushed images of the perfection of the female form that are so rife in today's culture.

After graduating with a fine art degree, Kat achieved a successful full-time teaching career for 14 years, and continues to teach art part-time whilst passionately pursuing her mission of world domination by empowering as many women as possible to reach their fullest potential by embracing their bodies and loving themselves wholeheartedly. Kat spreads her inspirational magic through her artwork, her Wellbeing business "Fabulously Imperfect", and her dedication to Goddess energy.

Reiki is a huge part of her life, and as a Reiki Master, Kat is committed to sharing Reiki, teaching Usui, Angelic and Karuna Reiki, and channelling Reiki energy through her artwork to uplift and heal.

As a Sister of Avalon, Kat also works directly with her Goddess consciousness, connecting to Goddess and Priestess energy and translating it into Divine Feminine infused paintings to inspire women and spread Goddess love.

Kat is also mum to a gorgeous teenage daughter, a bellydancer and an avid pioneer to improve the lives of rescue animals.

Kay Louise Aldred is a researcher, writer, and educator, who catalyses individual, institutional and collective evolution – through education, embodiment, and creativity – amalgamating metacognition, intuition, and instinct.

She has published three workbooks of her own with Girl God Books – *Mentorship of Goddess: Growing Sacred Womanhood, Making Love with the Divine: Sacred, Ecstatic, Erotic Experiences* and *Somatic Shamanism: Your Fleshy Knowing as the Tree of Life* – in addition to co-authoring *Embodied Education: Creating Safe Space for Learning Facilitating and Sharing* with her husband Dan Aldred. The couple reside in North Yorkshire, England.

www.kaylouisealdred.com
Instagram, Twitter and LinkedIn @kaylouisealdred

Liz Darling is a visual artist known for cosmic, organic paintings that often feature fungi, lunar imagery, and the female body. With a precise, organized approach and a personal emphasis on process and exploration, Liz uses watercolor, ink, and various other media to engage the intersection of magic, nature, the divine feminine, and the inner child. Liz exhibits her work in various gallery shows, festivals, markets, and publications. She is a member of the Joplin Regional Artists' Coalition, a frequent contributor to the *We'Moon* astrological datebook, and her work appears on the film sets of the HBO show *Mrs. Fletcher* and Hulu's *Sex Appeal*. In addition to making art, she enjoys hiking, documenting beautiful things in nature, traveling with her family, playing music, and walking her beloved dog, Oro. Liz lives and works in Pittsburg, KS, surrounded by the prairie and wide Kansas sky.

Louise Wisechild is a singer and songwriter offering songs of empowerment, courage, spirit and social justice. She is also the author of two memoirs, *The Obsidian Mirror: An Adult Healing from Incest* and *The Mother I Carry: Healing from Emotional Abuse* – as well as the editor of an anthology on healing from incest through art, *She Who Was Lost Is Remembered*. Louise lives in a Maya pueblo in Guatemala with three cats where she offers Guatemala Festival and Cultural tours as well as on-line tarot readings and creative life coaching.

Manya Kapikian is a student of the Temple of Witchcraft Mystery School. In her free time, Manya collects rocks, plants and surrounds herself with crystals, cats and some truly wonderful characters of life.

Mary Saracino is a novelist, poet, and memoir writer who lives in New Mexico. Her most recent novel is Heretics: A Love Story

(Pearlsong Press 2014). Her novel, The Singing of Swans (Pearlsong Press 2006) was a 2007 Lambda Literary Awards Finalist. She is also the author of the novels, *No Matter What* and *Finding Grace*, and the memoir *Voices of the Soft-bellied Warrior*. Mary's short story, "Vicky's Secret," earned the 2007 Glass Woman Prize. Her poetry and shorter fiction and creative nonfiction pieces have been published in a variety of literary and cultural journals and anthologies, both online and in print. For more information www.marysaracino.com.

Maya Luna is a Poet and teacher of the Lost Feminine Wisdom Streams. She teaches online and worldwide and is the creator of the *Deep Feminine Mystery School*. She offers gateways into feminine ways of knowing and perceiving reality. Her first book of poetry, *OMEGA: Feral Secrets of the Deep Feminine* is available on Amazon, and her spoken word album, *Holy Darkness: A Tantric Opus*, is streaming on all major platforms. Her second poetry and music album, *Holy Grail*, will be released this year.

Melisa Ann Howarth, born and raised in central Massachusetts, is a poet and self-evolution writer. She began writing poetry at the young age of 12, as a way of processing the difficult chronic health issues she was dealt with in her life. At the age of 35, after going through a spiritual awakening which resulted in profound self-transformation, she began to self-publish her poetry and other motivational writings on social media platforms. At 37, after completing a series of holistic and esoteric trainings and certifications, she took interest in writing guided meditations for others who walk a similar path of whole-being wellness and intentional living.

You can follow her writing content on Instagram @danceswithlightandshadow, as well as follow on Facebook at https://www.facebook.com/melisa.howarth/

Molly Remer, MSW, D.Min, is a priestess facilitating women's circles, seasonal rituals, and family ceremonies in central Missouri.

Molly and her husband Mark co-create Story Goddesses at Brigid's Grove. Molly is the author of nine books, including *Walking with Persephone, Whole and Holy, Womanrunes,* and the *Goddess Devotional.* She is the creator of the devotional experience #30DaysofGoddess and she loves savoring small magic and everyday enchantment.

Nina Gyorgy is a 19-year-old former Boston College student raised in a small town in central Maine. Nina was raised in the church, but her family parted from religion in her youth and turned to more metaphysical solutions. She regularly speaks to psychics, reads tarot, meditates, and works with the ever-flowing energy that is available to all of us. Nina was salutatorian of her high school class and felt pressure to attend a well-ranked college to prove her worth through external means. Nina majored in Environmental Science and minored in Dance Performance while at BC. Nina now attends Ringerike Folkehøgskole for Dance while healing from assault and pursuing her interest of tarot by giving readings on TikTok @ninareadstarot. Nina looks forward to where life will take her in the year following Folkehøgskole and knows that wherever she goes she will continue to dance and search for her own answers to life through her connection to source energy and by following her intuitive spirit.

Pamela Genghini Munoz is an immigration attorney, ordained Universal Life Church clergy, and self-described eclectic witch on the U.S.-Mexico Border. She has been published in *Sage Woman Magazine*, appeared on the *Missing Witches Podcast*, and blogs about the intersection of feminism, spirituality, politics and the human experience at https://medium.com. Pamela lives in El Paso, Texas with her husband, son, and a zoo that includes 6 dogs, 3 turtles, 1 snake, 3 cats and countless fresh and saltwater creatures.

Pat Daly is a mother of three daughters and proud grandma. A published author / writer on career and job search issues, Pat lives in Portland, Oregon. She has edited all of the Girl God Books from the beginning.

Philomena van Rijswijk is a Tasmanian visual artist and author.

Rachael Noton is a figurative artist, focusing on the empowerment of the woman's body, having always loved colour in her art she uses it in such a way that is abstract and flowing, just as the woman's body is, free flowing and like a woman- dances. Rachael started off by intuitively painting and drawing, but now that she has been to college she uses her skills and knowledge as well as her intuition. Rachael feels drawn to spiritual art and loves the feeling of the unknown, so when she puts brush to canvas she is pulled in a direction that just isn't known yet, and her art is born.

Raine Shakti is a pro-choice advocate who believes that forcing women to have unwanted children does irreparable harm. She has a MA degree in Spirituality, Culture, and Health from Western Michigan University and is currently studying the impacts of religious beliefs on activism. She currently lives in OH and when she is not reading, researching, or advocating, she enjoys hanging out with her family and her two pit bulls.

Raven Bishop is a mother, daughter and sister; educator and creatrix. Her work as a ceremonialist artist finds her working closely with the element of fire, creating artworks, poetry, performance and rituals that foster personal growth and community building.

Ravynne Phelan, a.k.a. Michele-lee Phelan, has been painting since the year 2000. As a child, she dreamed of becoming an artist, but fell into a state of despair and confusion in her teenage years when many told her a career in art was an unattainable dream. Made vulnerable by mental illness, she believed this to be truth and laid down her brushes. For the next fourteen years she lived in a world of grey, empty of colour, dreams, and goals until she was officially diagnosed with depression and introduced to art as a form of emotional release and therapy.

This unconventional form of treatment rekindled the dreams of the child, and at 33 years of age, Ravynne took upon herself the mantle of professional artist and illustrator. She knew, with every fibre of her being, that some dreams are more than just dreams: they are destiny, and it was her destiny to become an artist and to share her journey and her message of magic, healing, and self-empowerment with others.

But this truth did not manifest as her reality until, after several years as a commercial artist and illustrator, Ravynne began to feel an emptiness once more. After much soul-searching, she came to understand that her creativity was meant to have more of a spiritual meaning and message. She dedicated herself to Great Spirit and Gaia and turned her back upon a growing career as a fantasy book-cover artist and children's book illustrator in order to first illustrate, and then to write and illustrate, oracle and tarot cards. From that moment, her life was transformed. Every artwork is now a collaborative endeavour between Ravynne, Great Spirit, and Gaia, and Ravynne has found herself on a path of healing and happiness Why? Because she has dared to live her dream.

As a professional illustrator, Ravynne – under the name of Michele-lee Phelan – has completed the cover artwork and internal illustrations for many publications, including the 'Oracle Of The Dragonfae' by Lucy Cavendish and 'Mythic Oracle' with Carisa Mellado (both from Blue Angel Publishing). Her book, the stunning 'Dreams of Magic' was her first solo publication and an expression of her blossoming creativity and love for the Divine.

In 2011, Michele-lee became Ravynne to celebrate and honour the magical path she has walked in service to Gaia and Great Spirit and to mark the end of her being defined by her past and mental illness. The Messenger Oracle was the second manifestation of her dreams of magic, and was released in 2012.

In 2015, Ravynne separated from her partner of 24 years and dedicated herself to her craft. From a new place of freedom and peace, she embraced her independence, asexuality and gender fluidity. In a space of growth and transition, she completed the long-awaited Dreams of Gaia Tarot which was released in July, 2016. This award-winning deck is one she considers to be her masterwork.

Since then, Ravynne has produced colouring books, journals, and in 2021, the magical sister deck to Messenger Oracle, Seeker Oracle, was created and sent out into the world. Ravynne is now working on a symbol-themed deck and a lenormand.

Website: https://www.ravynnephelan.com
Instagram: @ravynnephelan
Facebook: https://www.facebook.com/ravynnephelan

Reverend Rebecca Bryan is a Unitarian Universalist minister, a mother and a fierce advocate for justice and equity. Her journey of recovery from childhood sexual abuse and trauma forged her knowing that there is good within us all that no one can destroy, and that we all deserve a right to respect, freedom, self-expression and self-agency.

Reda Rackley, aka Bonewoman, is an internationally respected and loved teacher, oracle, diviner, mythologist, storyteller, writer, and "outsider artist".

Reda received her B.A. in Psychology with a special focus on Women's Spirituality. She graduated from Pacifica Graduate Institute in Santa Barbara with an M.A. in Mythology and Depth Psychology.

Reda, aka Bonewoman, embodies the wisdom of her ancestral Celtic granny witches, reading the bones, stones, and cowrie shells to peer into the otherworld to deliver messages from the ancestors, ancient ones, angels, and nature spirits.

She channels a nature spirit being that speaks in tongues, does automatic painting, and delivers healing vibrations from the unseen realms. She was blessed to travel to Burkina Faso with the late elder Malidoma some 25 years ago to become an initiated diviner and oracle. She has traveled internationally to offer her divinations and ritual healing work.

Renee Bedard is a witch, psychic, and a healing practitioner in Massachusetts. With a passion for storytelling, Renee weaves together myths and magick for her classes, guided meditations, rituals, and Goddess Circles. She believes that when we empower people to heal and find their voice, they can write their own story and understand who they are at their core. Renee enjoys writing about witchcraft, the Feminine Mysteries, and working with spirits for her blog, The Whispering Crow at thewhisperingcrow.com. She is also an Initiate in the Temple of Witchcraft tradition and is currently studying in the Mystery School for her fourth degree.

Sharon Smith is a writer, ghost writer, editor, and proofreader with a passion for helping women reconnect with their Authentic Selves and Voices. She loves and honors the Great Mother in all Her many forms and has a deep connection to Nature. She identifies as a Green Witch and follows an eclectic spiritual path that is a blending of Native American and Celtic Teachings, both in her ancestral line.

Sionainn McLean is a polytheist fire witch and animist, on a crazy spiritual journey over the last 25 years. She is a priestess of The Morrigan and has served the Great Queen for over 5 years. A recent graduate of the Community Ministry program with Cherry Hill Seminary, she is also working towards her spiritual direction certificate. She is the owner and operator of Liminal Raven Ministries whose mission is to aid in self-empowerment, provide inspiration, guidance, support, and ministry to pagans as well as to nurture spiritual growth in others. She's also a mom, wife, writer, painter and gardener.

Trista Hendren founded Girl God Books in 2011 to support a necessary unraveling of the patriarchal worldview of divinity. Her first book—*The Girl God*, a children's picture book—was a response to her own daughter's inability to see herself reflected in the divine. Since then, she has published more than 50 books with hundreds of contributors from across the globe. Originally from Portland, Oregon, she now lives in Bergen, Norway. You can learn more about her projects at www.thegirlgod.com

Arlene's Acknowledgments

I want to acknowledge with gratitude all the women who have been my mentors and teachers through the years that both inspired and taught me as I reclaimed Women's Herstory and Women's Ways and stepped into the roles of Priestess and Medicine Woman, Author and Artist, Oracle and Witch, Mentor and Teacher. It is also with incredible humility that I offer deep gratitude to those women who came to me as students to learn and reclaim women's ancient ways and then went out and amplified their skills and offerings to new groups of women.

As for this particular anthology… Such deeply intimate stories and ideas fill this antidote to patriarchal control and manipulation of all things female. It is truth-telling and raw, inspiring and at times fiercely personal. Always the stories from women that span the globe, age and background hold us in this crucible of change-making Herstory! To all our Contributors I say "Brava" for the women you are and the women you are becoming as you find your own path back to Her. May we walk hand in hand and heart in heart as we rage against this machine that would see us in chains and servitude.

With an open and grateful heart, I offer deep gratitude to Trista Hendren. From my first submission as a Contributor to this now as an Editor, you have been my champion and my support, my beloved friend and sister of the heart. We have followed many paths and gone down many rabbit holes and I have loved every minute of it as we have listened and discussed ideas and possibilities – sometimes in agreement, sometimes not – but always with honor and respect!! Here's to the future as we forge new pathways of dismantling patriarchy while elevating women and women's rights. May the work You/I/We do be in service to Goddess as we Re-member Her time and ways along with the Circle and our Ancient Lineage of Women's Ways of Being and Knowing, Living and Doing.

To my sister editors, Pat Daly and Sharon Smith, I say thank you for walking with me on this particular journey. Your guidance and wisdom have been invaluable, and I honor the women you are. Finally... From my heart, I also want to acknowledge and honor my beloved partner of 50 years who, in 2021, became an Ancestor. I met Larry my first night at university and throughout our journey – him as a Professor of Sociology with specialties in many things, including gender studies and me as an Anthropologist specializing in women's health care in undeveloped regions of the world – we unlearned our deep Southern Baptist inculturation and re-imagined our lives as activists and sovereign beings – both individually and collectively! No matter what I wanted to do or where I wanted to work in the world, he both supported and championed me and my choices. I am the woman I am today, in part, because of his incredible encouragement and support for any and everything I wanted to be and do!

Moving forward... To all of you and, indeed, all women, may the Chalice from which we drink fill us with the gnosis for the coming times. Blessed Be.

Sharon's Acknowledgments

I'd like to dedicate this anthology, first of all, to my 10th Great-Grandmother on two conjoined lines of my Family Tree: Margaret Stephenson Scott, who was hanged by the neck until dead, 22 September 1692, during the insanity of the Salem Witch Trials, at around 73 years of age, because she refused to bow the knee to the patriarchs of her local church and government and "come under the authority of a man" after her husband died in his 50s. She remained a single and sovereign woman for nearly 20 years at a time when men feared such "rebelliousness" in females; so, of course, when she was old and it fell to the Church to take care of her under their "widows and orphans," teaching, it was far more profitable for the

Church to declare her a "witch" and thus eliminate her "rebellious example." Grandmother Margaret, to me, is an early example of a Woman who paid the ultimate price for her sovereignty: Death at the hands of patriarchal men. She is a true Shero to me, and I am honored to be her Granddaughter!

I would also like to dedicate this anthology to all the Women down through HIStory who have made HERstory known, through their courageous acts of rebellion against the misogyny of Patriarchy: all who have fought the system, spoken their truths, actively worked for and reclaimed aspects of their Divine Feminine Sovereignty, and, thus, paved the way for all of us Women today, to carry the torch forward. You are Loved. You are Remembered. You are Honored!

To my Sister Editors and Writers, Pat Daly, Arlene Bailey, and Trista Hendren: WOW! What a Journey this has been, Beloveds! I am so honored to have walked it with you all. You are such shining lights in this world for Women everywhere. May you be blessed beyond measure! I love and deeply respect you all!

To my daughters, Colleen and Kelinda, and to my granddaughters, Abby and Danika; to my niece Rachelle and my great-niece Aubree, and my heart-daughters, Angie Metzner and Renee Jamerson, thank you all for being in my life and bringing me so much joy; and also for your loving support and, quite simply, just your love: I am blessed beyond measure by each one of you. This is for you, that this world may be a better one for each and every one of you amazing Women (and Women-in-Training). I see you. I Honor you. I love you!

And finally, to my "Big Bro," Robert Roffman, my dear friend and fellow Edgewalker in this life: a Sacred Masculine—and a Magickal—Man, who has always been there to support me on my Spiritual Journey. A fellow Earth-connected Soul, an exceptionally talented Nature photographer, who listens to Trees and Waterfalls, loves and works with Horses, and who has found acceptance among the Elementals of the Deep Forests, Bob is a staunch supporter of Women's Rights and advocates for us whenever and however he can. I thank him for that unflinching support, and for sharing his Magickal Moments with me through phones calls from time to time. Bro, you give us hope for Mankind! Much Love and Many Blessings to you!

Trista's Acknowledgments

I would like to acknowledge my co-editors. My mother, **Pat Daly,** has edited each and every one of my books. There would be no Girl God Books without her enormous contributions. I was thrilled to work with my beloved Sisters, **Arlene Bailey** and **Sharon Smith,** on this project as well. Thank you both so much for your attention to detail and support of this work for so many years. I love all three of you!

Tremendous gratitude to **Ravynne M Phelan** for allowing us to feature her gorgeous painting as the cover art.

Enormous appreciation to my husband **Anders Løberg**, who prepared the document for printing and helped with website updates. Your love, support and many contributions made this book possible.

Lastly, I would like to thank my dear sisters **Tamara Albanna, Susan Morgaine, Kay Louise Aldred, Sharon Smith, Arlene Bailey, Arna Baartz, Kat Shaw, Jessica Bahr** and **Alyscia Cunningham** for always being right there to cheer me on in the spirit of true sisterhood.

Thank you to all our readers and Girl God supporters over the years. We love and appreciate you!

If you enjoyed this book, please consider writing a brief review on StoryGraph, Amazon, and/or Goodreads.

What's Next?!

Asherah: Roots of the Mother Tree – Edited by Claire Dorey, Janet Rudolph, Pat Daly and Trista Hendren

The Wisdom of Cerridwen: Transforming in Her Cosmic Brew – Edited by Emma Clark, Trista Hendren, and Pat Daly

Lady of the Forge: Stories and Art Dedicated to the Goddess Brigid – Edited by Isca Johnson, Trista Hendren, and Pat Daly

Kali Rising: Holy Rage – Edited by C. Ara Campbell, Jaclyn Cherie, Trista Hendren, and Pat Daly

Pain Perspectives: Finding Meaning in the Fire – Edited by Kay Turner, Trista Hendren and Pat Daly

Wounded Feminine: Grieving with Goddess – Edited by Claire Dorey, Trista Hendren, and Pat Daly

Sacred Breasts: an Inspirational Anthology for Living Your Breast Life – Edited by Barbara O'Meara, Trista Hendren, and Pat Daly